A1/89. ML

THE
COUNTRY CHAPEL

Of like interest:
The Country Bus
The Country Railway
The Country Canal (in preparation)

THE
COUNTRY CHAPEL

John Hibbs

David & Charles
Newton Abbot   London   North Pomfret (Vt)

*Photographs are from the author's collection
unless stated otherwise*

Copyright Notice

The author thanks all who have assisted by giving permission to use material under the laws of copyright, as follows: Mr Nathaniel Micklem for the passage from *Congregationalism and the Church Catholic*, by Revd Dr N Micklem; Mr Michael Williams and Messrs David Higham Associates for the passage from *The Place of the Lion*, by Charles Williams; Mr Cyril Jolly for the print of 'God's Cottage'; Mr Robert Roskrow for the print of 'Come to Good'; Mr E Gower for the drawing of Grassington Congregational Church; and the Ordnance Survey for the map showing Providence Chapel, on pages 60 & 61. For the extracts from S L Bensusan's books I have been unable to trace the owners of copyright, but Mr John Bensusan-Butt has assured me that there need be no obstacle to their reproduction. The author and publishers would apologise to any other owner of copyright whose material has been reproduced without authority, and will happily amend this record in any future edition of the book.

British Library Cataloguing in Publication Data

Hibbs, John
    The country chapel.
    1. Great Britain, Rural regions. Chapels. Social aspects, to 1987.
    I. Title
    306'.6'0941
    ISBN 0–7153–8960–2

Phototypeset by ABM Typographics Limited Hull
and printed in Great Britain
by Butler & Tanner Limited Frome
for David & Charles Publishers plc
Brunel House   Newton Abbot   Devon

Published in the United States of America
by David & Charles Inc
North Pomfret   Vermont 05053   USA

'Go into all the world . . .' (Mark 16, V15, RSV)

• Contents •

◆ Foreword ◆

I WAS intrigued by this delightful result of detailed research. I have always been an espouser – not of lost causes, because the Christian Church is never that – but of problem churches. I don't believe in churches closing down and buildings being sold. It looks like a lack of faith in the future. So several times I have been able to bring a little weight to bear on the side of renewal. The lovely old chapel at Chulmleigh, in Devon, the oldest after Horningsham, was reduced to nine members. I asked them if they would like me to minister there for six months. I stayed two and a half years – part-time – and then was able to introduce the Revd Elaine Marsh BD, just retired from a 2,000-strong church in Minneapolis. She came for six months. One might say she came and saw and conquered – and was conquered; she loved Chulmleigh church and its people and the Westcountry so much that she has sold a beautiful home in Minneapolis in order to stay here. The membership now stands at almost forty! I think Elaine has brought back to Chulmleigh something of the community sense that the American churches have.

The sense of the larger family and the community has tended to be lost to British churches, while the spirit of independency, the basis of so many of the chapels, has languished, and 'waiting on the Holy Spirit', the purpose of the Congregational and Baptist church meeting, has been neglected. In this age of the big battalions, when audiences for TV are numbered in millions, we need desperately to recapture the personal responsibility for discovering the mind of Christ and working out His will in the family of the Church and the wider community.

I am proud of my own now small denomination, that has chosen to remain Congregational and independent. And I rejoice in the new breed of men and women, some from quite small chapels, who have taken up studies laid down by the denomination that may lead to ministerial training. There are already many fully trained non-stipendary ministers, who are building up the church in small towns and villages that could not afford a full-time minister.

So I hope that the traditions so admirably sought out and described by Dr Hibbs in this book will be rejuvenated and renewed to meet the modern need for community and simplicity and Christian morality. 'Being the Church' is finding ways of sharing and spreading the Gospel. William Temple said 'The Church is the only institution that exists for the benefit of its non-members'. The independency of the country chapels upholds the responsibility of every member to see to that. May they be revived and renewed to meet the need for a new sort of puritanism in modern living. And may *The Country Chapel* add fuel to the fire of the Spirit.

Revd Elsie Chamberlain BD
Minister, Castle Gate Centre, Nottingham;
Past Chairman of Council,
The Congregational Federation

1

◊ Introduction ◊

THE closing hymn has been given out by the preacher; the congregation stands, and the organist plays through the first two lines of the tune that everyone knows: 'The day Thou gavest, Lord, is ended'. Then, with the opening chord repeated, the singing starts. The sound that rises in the chapel is far from the measured cadences of a great cathedral choir, but it is of full volume, reasonably rhythmical, and above all, it is the sound of people who feel what they are singing. For them, the darkness falls with no attempt to extend daylight by street lamps and brightly lit shops. Life is closer to nature than that, so it is natural to go on with the hymn, and sing: 'The darkness falls at Thy behest'. And as the last verse swells to the double forte marked in the hymn-book, there is feeling too in the words: 'Thy throne shall never, Like earth's proud empires, pass away'. What we can hear is not just the voice of country people, living with the seasons and the land; it is also the voice of dissent.

Before the service began we had time to look round at the building. Bare walls, bare beams overhead, rounded windows filled with plain glass, letting in the last of the daylight of an evening in late spring. Pews painted brown and varnished, with bare boards beneath, divided into three blocks by aisles where there are coloured tiles on the floor. In front of us the pulpit is set centrally against the wall, with a short flight of stairs, complete with banisters and handrails, leading to it from either side, and, set below the pulpit on a dais, a small table, with a brass vase of flowers on it, is surrounded by five chairs.

Outside, the building can only be called homely, though it has some aspirations to style. It is not very old; perhaps late nineteenth century at the earliest; but it is not the age of the building that matters, for there has been a dissenting congregation worshipping in this village since the late eighteenth century, when it was established by followers of Selina, Countess of Huntingdon. At first associated with Methodism, the Countess of Huntingdon's Connexion, always one of the smaller nonconformist sects, remained firmly Calvinistic as the main Methodist

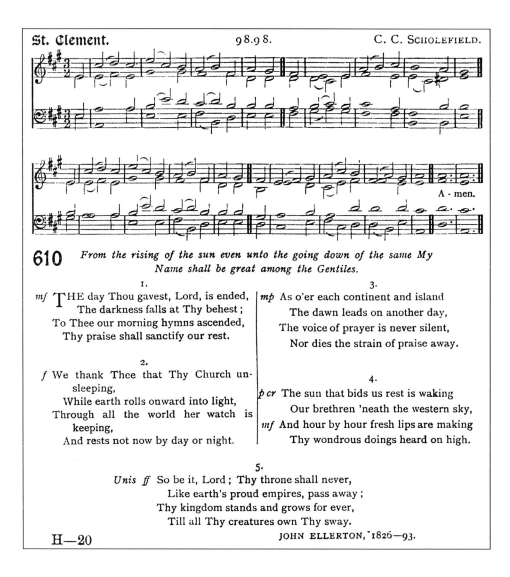

St. Clement.   98.98.   C. C. SCHOLEFIELD.

A - men.

610 *From the rising of the sun even unto the going down of the same My Name shall be great among the Gentiles.*

1.

mf THE day Thou gavest, Lord, is ended,
The darkness falls at Thy behest;
To Thee our morning hymns ascended,
Thy praise shall sanctify our rest.

2.

f We thank Thee that Thy Church un-
sleeping,
While earth rolls onward into light,
Through all the world her watch is
keeping,
And rests not now by day or night.

3.

mp As o'er each continent and island
The dawn leads on another day,
The voice of prayer is never silent,
Nor dies the strain of praise away.

4.

p cr The sun that bids us rest is waking
Our brethren 'neath the western sky,
mf And hour by hour fresh lips are making
Thy wondrous doings heard on high.

5.

Unis ff So be it, Lord; Thy throne shall never,
Like earth's proud empires, pass away;
Thy kingdom stands and grows for ever,
Till all Thy creatures own Thy sway.

H—20   JOHN ELLERTON, 1826—93.

tradition moved with Wesley to a rather less fatalistic belief, and came to be associated with the Congregationalists. So this evening we are in the very heart of dissent, and though the village is in the English shires, the chapel traces its origins from the college founded by the Countess at Trevecca, in South Wales. (Today the pulpit and brass candelabra from the Countess's own chapel are still in use in Oat Hall Chapel, at Wivelsfield, in Sussex.)

When we came in we were given a hymn-book by the sidesman, but no prayer book, and no printed order of service. Truth to tell, the sidesman was a little embarrassed at the arrival of strangers, but he greeted us with a smile and handshake, and showed us to a pew, before hurrying back to his post in the vestibule. Since everyone clearly knew what to expect, the form of the service was not lightly to be changed. A notice outside, which gave the name of the pastor and the secretary, had told us that this evening the preacher is a layman, and we have joined in the hymns, listened to the Bible reading and the notices, and shared in the extempore prayers, sitting in silence with head bowed – no kneeling here.

Gas lights had been lit before we arrived, and as the daylight faded outside, the chapel became more and more an island of faith and serenity, as moving in its way as the atmosphere at evensong in the fourteenth-century parish church at the other end of the village. The darkness outside was complete as the preacher gave out his text, and the congregation settled down to the central part of the service, the sermon. Preaching from Isaiah Chapter 6, Verse 1, 'In the year that King Uzziah died I saw the Lord . . .', the preacher stressed the reality of religious experience, capable

Selina, Countess of Huntingdon, originated more than 200 years ago the 'Connexion' to which this Hertfordshire chapel belongs. Cardinal Newman said of her 'she sets Christians of all times an example'.

In dissent, the sermon is the climax of the service, so the pulpit replaces the altar as the centrepiece of the building – as here, in Horningsham Old Meeting (the earliest nonconformist chapel of them all).

of being dated like that, and took us through some examples from literature and biography that spoke of no narrow or circumscribed culture. In the silence the congregation seemed to weigh his thoughts and for almost twenty minutes everyone's attention was focussed on the hearing of the Word.

But the service is ending now. We remain standing after the hymn is finished to hear the blessing, and then sit in silent prayer until the organist begins the final voluntary. Then, as the preacher comes down from the pulpit and walks to the back, people begin to busy themselves with conversation, and follow him to the doors. There is handshaking, and . enquiries after relatives, and several words of thanks for the sermon. Gradually the congregation disperses, walking home through the lanes – for this is 1943, and few cars are about. Men and women are returning to cottages, some to larger farms, or to council houses, united by shared faith and worship. Theirs is a community, with roots deep in the past, and traditions that are still alive.

There is a board in front of the building, with the name of the chapel, and the following information –

> Services: SUNDAY 11.00 A.M.
> 6.30 P.M.
> SUNDAY SCHOOL 9.45 A.M.
> WEEKNIGHT BIBLE STUDY AND
> PRAYER MEETING — WEDNESDAY 7.15 P.M.

If we could consult the denominational 'Year Book', we might find a little statistical evidence of the community – thirty-five 'church members', twenty 'scholars' in the Sunday School, with the date of the foundation and the names of minister and church secretary. If we came to know the village, we would discover the annual events that are the high points of the year for the congregation, and for others too – the Sunday School Anniversary, with special services morning and evening; the Sunday School Treat, which is an outing for the children; the Harvest Festival, which has more meaning here than it has in many city churches or chapels. We would follow the minister in his round of visits, his acts of quiet charity, and his slightly ambiguous relationship with the Anglican parson, on the one hand, and with the untrained, but enormously sincere pastor of the evangelical tabernacle on the other.

And we would come to understand the people of the chapel. Mainly middle-aged or elderly; mainly lower middle class or working class; rather more women than men; they vary in devotion from the regular 'twicers', attending morning and evening every week, to the more spasmodic supporters. In addition, there are the village people who send their children to the Sunday School, but who will only be seen in the pews when it comes round to the anniversary, or perhaps for harvest. Supporting the minister there will be the secretary, the treasurer, and a group elected from the members to the office of deacon; these with the organist and the caretaker will be the core of the chapel community. For them, the chapel is the centre of their lives.

The British have never been famous for consistency, and we have already seen that there is some ambiguity in the use of the words church and chapel. Not surprisingly, nonconformity regards itself as part of the Christian Church, and this may account for the importance of 'church membership', to which you are admitted 'on profession of faith', usually at an age when it is reckoned you understand what it means – about fifteen, perhaps. The title 'Church Secretary' is often used, too. But there is, even in these ecumenical days, something distinguishable about 'being chapel', and it is that which gives strength and cohesion to these small communities.

To say that it is a social identity in no way diminishes its religious – indeed its theological – significance. Though many who worship in the parish church may be 'villagers' (itself a term redolent of social class), the parson and churchwardens will be drawn from that group known as the 'residents', whose social position is indicated by their names appearing in the county directory. In the chapel you would expect to find the tradesmen and their wives, perhaps the station-master, and a good many of the farmworkers too. Independence of character combined with a sense of self-respect, has always been part of the chapel tradition.

In areas where small farmers were common, a man might sit among his labourers on a Sunday, but where farms were bigger, and farmers aspired to a higher social standing, the labourers would be self-consciously chapel. 'It's none of 'is business where I goes on Sundays,' a man might say; 'I don't 'ave to do 'is bidding seven days a week.' In parts of Norfolk, less than a generation ago, the local organiser of the National Union of Agricultural Workers used to meet his members and do much of his routine business outside the Methodist chapel after Sunday morning service. That was where he knew he could expect to find his people. In the pit villages of the northern coalfields this was carried to still greater lengths, the chapel being the social centre of what were very much one-class communities.

For the tradespeople and the lower middle class, chapel was also an escape from problems of social relationships, and a place where they could feel that they were among their own kind. Along with this went a sense of independence, necessary perhaps for self-respect. Constance Holme, the Westmorland novelist, in *Crump Folk Going Home*, makes a labourer compete with the squire in a wrestling match, and almost kill him, by accident. Far from praising his win, the lad's parents are disgusted with him – 'hate Crump, but leave it alone' is their philosophy. So it has been for centuries with chapel folk, who have found in their own institutions a refuge from the overbearing attitudes of the gentry.

The ancestry of chapel folk lies too in the attitudes of the establishment to the followers of John Wesley and his fellow preachers. The eighteenth century Duchess of Buckingham, Silvester Horne tells us, 'was highly disgusted at the Methodist assumption that "there is no distinction of persons" before God, and that *all* have sinned and come short of His glory. "It is monstrous," she said, "to be told that you have a heart as sinful as the common wretches that crawl upon the earth." ' Away and behind that there is the persecution that was suffered by dissent – Catholic and Protestant alike – after the Restoration, and the emergence of an alliance between nonconformity and the Liberal Party in the nineteenth century. All in all, the awareness of 'being chapel' is rooted deep in the social and political history of the nation.

There are other, more recognisable differences, too. We have already seen the kind of building that is characteristic of a nonconformist chapel, more especially in the villages. (There are great examples of nineteenth-century Gothic architecture in many urban churches of the dissenting

Between Monmouth and Abergavenny, the Methodist chapel at Wernhoellydd displays the simplicity of the country chapel at its best. *(Mrs V Townsend)*

tradition, as well as of the plain good looks recognised for us by Pevsner.) The typical village chapel runs to extreme plainness, as if any vestige of ecclesiastical design was to be avoided; some resemble barns, which is perhaps where the first assemblies took place locally; others are domestic, even to the extent of the chapel at Gressenhall in Norfolk, which is known as 'God's Cottage'.

There is no doubt that architectural style reflects a tradition closer to that of the Quakers than it is to the established church. The term 'meeting house' comes to mind as readily for many of these buildings as that of 'chapel', and 'going to meeting' is a phrase as acceptable in the chapel tradition as much as that of the Quakers – indeed, the expression 'best Sunday-go-to-meeting suit' was to be heard in the present author's Essex childhood. What mattered was a style that in no way resembled the buildings castigated in Bunyan's use of the term 'steeple houses'.

But the importance of design lies as much inside the chapel as it does in the external architecture. The place of the pulpit, centrally against the end wall, rarely if ever departed from in the traditional dissenting chapel, is significant of the central place of the 'teaching ministry' – it has been said that the sermon takes the place of the raising of the Host in Roman ritual,

Simplicity marks the chapel interior, too. Here in the Bedfordshire village of Renhold are the traditional hard benches, varnished woodwork, and the text that expresses the faith of the chapel. *(Mr F G Smith)*

as the central point of the service. This, as we shall see, is linked to the importance of an educated clergy, alongside the equal stress upon the lay pastorate. It may have the slightly ludicrous consequence that the congregation appears to worship the choir, if, as is often the case, the singers are placed in front of the pulpit.

When a communion service is held, which in the main tradition of dissent is likely to be on the first Sunday of the month, the minister descends from the pulpit and officiates from the table, where he sits facing the congregation. In this may be seen a conscious refusal of the sacerdotal principle long accepted in the Roman and High Anglican Churches, which in nonconformist dissent is replaced by the 'priesthood of all believers'. Less generally, and only in the chapels of the evangelical sects that have often had a strong rural background, there may be a 'testimony bench', where individuals can sit, facing the congregation, and recall the circumstances of their conversion, among cries of 'Hallelujah' and 'praise the Lord'.

The differences between the various nonconformist sects have deeper roots than might at first appear, when there is so much in common where their forms of worship are concerned. One reason why the smaller chapels, and thus the country chapels almost by definition, have a fixed order of service, despite the general dislike of 'prayer-book services' among their adherents, may be a mixture of poverty and poor education among past generations. For a congregation that could not have afforded printed service leaflets, even if they could have been widely read, it was simplest for the order of service to remain unchanged, subject only to the numbers of the hymns being displayed on a bracket on the wall.

This is born out by the recorded knowledge that even hymn-books are a relatively recent innovation. It was common practice for the minister to read the hymns, a few lines or a verse at a time, after which he and the congregation joined in singing what he had just read. The story goes that on one evening, the minister felt constrained to remark that –

> The light is growing very dim,
> I scarce can see to read the hymn.

– whereupon the audience sang his words. At this he admonished them, saying –

> I did not mean to read the hymn,
> I simply said the light was dim.

– and so they sang that, too. But as to the truth of that tale, who can tell?

2

⋄ Dissent and the Parish ⋄

IN villages and country towns the word 'chapel' has come to have several layers of meaning, quite apart from the actual building. Indeed, many chapels have boards outside them announcing them to be churches, while others have kept to the traditional term 'meeting house', which is far from being limited to the Society of Friends. But while the origins of dissent lie in matters of serious doctrinal and theological significance, there are social aspects to the chapel, that continue to be important in many communities today.

To be 'chapel' is to be different. In Wales the difference has been partly nationalistic, but it has had social implications as well, in a society where the upper class was seen to be representative of the alien, English culture. But in England there are social aspects to being chapel, too. The Anglican parish church could command the allegiance of the squirearchy and of some at least of the professional or retired people resident in the village; of the people who might today be called 'establishment', just as their church is established in the state. Not for nothing has the Church of England been called 'the Tory Party on its knees'. Nevertheless, the parish clergy for long tended to assume that if the villagers were not also parishioners, then they ought to be; and, of course, many of them were. In our consideration of the chapel and all that it means in rural society, we must never forget the devoted service to the parish church that has been given by people of every social class.

But there have always been others, for whom the established church could never be their home. The British are an independent race, and do not take easily to being 'kept in their place'. There is an irony behind Dickens' quatrain, in *The Chimes*, that expresses all that the independent-minded people of these islands feel –

> *O let us love our occupations,*
> *Bless the squire and his relations,*
> *Live upon our daily rations,*
> *And always know our proper stations.*

A nineteenth-century formality makes the Wesleyan chapel at Spridlington in Lincolnshire look almost urban in its architecture. (*Mr J R Marshall*)

To that your Britishman says 'no thanks', and sets about building his own social structure, where no one can order him about. And that has been an important part of his attitude to the state church that claims his allegiance, to the extent that he will be officially labelled 'C of E' unless he goes out of his way to establish himself as a nonconformist or Catholic dissenter.

Sometimes, though, he is forced into it. The Lincolnshire village of Spridlington had a population of about 250 when the Methodist chapel was opened at the start of this century, and Mr J R Marshall contributes this reminiscence, which he had from someone who was involved in its establishment.

> . . . as a boy, he was in the Anglican Church choir in the village, for it was the general practice to attend Anglican Church services in the morning and the Wesleyan Methodist service in the evening . . . The Vicar at that time would be a Revd. Hutton, a member of a substantial land-owning family in the county, and who seems to have acted almost as a semi-squire in the parish as well as the incumbent. Somewhere around 1900 a new Vicar , a Revd. Page, was appointed, who made drastic changes in the village practice, demanding

in effect that the villagers make a choice of adherence to the Anglican or the Methodist Church, since he inaugurated an Anglican evening service. The Taylor clan – there were quite a number of them – seem to have all opted for the Methodist Church, and I am guessing that this had something to do with the go-ahead to build the new chapel.

There is a specially sad touch to this story, which crops up in several of the contributions to this book, where people were forced to choose, and had to give up the musical life of the Anglican Church in order to remain faithful to their dissenting beliefs. That there is a social, not to say an economic aspect to all this cannot be denied. The freedom to improve yourself, or your children, by 'getting on' is deeply engrained in our society, and must have meant for many a resentment for the words of the prayer book about 'the station in life to which it has pleased God to call us'. But it is also the case that knowing your place in society has meant a mutual respect – the squire's lady might be shown into the parlour, but in comparison it was the favoured few that received the hospitality of the kitchen. And the squire's lady was expected to know *her* station, and not seek to stray from the parlour.

Thus being chapel meant that you kept your place in society in worship as well as work. You shopped in different places from the residents, whose goods were delivered to their homes, anyway. Until the great changes of the mid-twentieth century, and perhaps to some extent today, the country chapel was a necessary part of the rural social structure, giving comfort and self-respect to many who were still expected to raise their hats to their superiors, and earn a labourer's meagre wage.

But to limit the significance of chapel to that would be to ignore the faith and intelligence of the chapel-goer. We shall see that the tradition of dissent goes back to deep and strongly held convictions as to doctrine, and while no doubt a minority of any chapel congregation could articulate their beliefs, that must never be seen to imply that their beliefs were not understood. Through the eighteenth and nineteenth centuries, and into the twentieth, many nonconformist clergy had a better theological education than many of their brethren in the established church – before the reform of the universities, the dissenting academies gave them for the most part a better general education too. This, combined with the central importance of the sermon, meant that chapel folk were in receipt of more than mere piety in their services, and it would be an insult to suggest that, because they might not be able to explain in their own words what the preacher had said in his sermon, it had meant nothing to them.

But so far we have tended to see a simple divide between chapel and the parish church, which is a gross over-simplification. Even now, in small country towns and the larger villages, there will be two or more chapels of different denominations, and a century ago this was even more true. We shall see in chapter five the distinctions in dissent that produced this richness of doctrine and worship, but for the moment we must remember the further social divisions that have marked the life of rural non-conformity.

S L Bensusan, who knew the religion of the Essex marshland folk as well as he did their working world and their homes and leisure, has many pictures of evangelical congregations sitting under a pastor who might be the local carrier, and who took a great personal care for the spiritual welfare of his flock. But Bensusan was fond of describing the marshland as 'back of beyond', and he lacks the distinction that can mean so much, between these gatherings of unlettered (but very sincere) believers, and the chapels of the Methodists, Baptists and Congregationalists, with their paid clergy and loose or strong national organisations. In their places of worship might be found the tradespeople of the village, as well as the labouring class; still more so would this be true in the small country towns.

For the success of the country chapel depended very much upon the availability of local leadership. Not for these congregations was there the possibility of a parson, appointed by the owner of the living, who might (or might not) bring inspiration to their faith, and organisation to their lives. The evangelical sects of the nineteenth century grew from the personal conviction of men and women who had experienced conversion, but they seldom had even part payment for their leaders – the word 'clergy' would be quite out of place here. For the older denominations, where a stipend would be expected for the minister, however small that payment might be, there were usually a few middle-class people to share in the organisation, and the larger villages would have had tailors and carpenters as well as farmers living on the land they farmed, from whom such support for the cause might come. The chapel congregation, then, was socially more extensive; we can almost distinguish three strands in village religion – the Anglican, the nonconformist and the evangelical.

Of the three, it seems that the first and last have survived best into the late twentieth century. The process of change is not new, but it is closely associated with changes in agriculture, and these take us back a hundred years, for as early as 1876 John Clifford was reporting the 'decay' of non-conformist chapels in his book *Religious Life in the Rural Districts of England*.

Mechanisation was driving men from the land, and it was often those with 'fidelity to conscience' that went first; they had been independent-minded chapel folk. The great depression of the late nineteenth century meant that wages were cut, especially in East Anglia, which from the Civil War onward had been a great homeland of dissent. But above all, as the radical traditions of dissent affected their labourers, the farmers tended to desert the chapels, and with them, too often, went the organising ability needed for survival.

Of course there were many exceptions, and the rural chapels survived and in many places flourished. Independent tradesmen might fill the gap left by the farmers, whose upward social mobility presumably took them to the parish church. But the virtual collapse of arable farming between the two great wars of the twentieth century repeated the pattern of the previous generation, and the radical changes in agriculture since 1945 have had perhaps the greatest impact of all. For today the agricultural labourer is the least likely person you would expect to meet in the village, and the labourers' cottages now are too often second homes for incomers from the towns. Those who once supported the country chapel are among the thousands who have left the land.

The country chapel in Wales, with its very different social structure, has had a different place, and the same can be said of Cornwall. Here the great revival of the eighteenth century left the lasting influence of Methodism, though its importance for the English villages must not be neglected in comparison. In Wales the chapel became the principal place of worship, a fact recognised by the disestablishment of the Anglican Church in Wales in 1920; in the Westcountry Methodism became so well established that the Bible Christians after 1817 became a separate denomination, after William O'Bryan, their founder, had been 'excluded' from Methodism. The strength of faith and practice among the Westcountry sects is illustrated for us by Betjeman's reference to these people, a century later, in *Summoned by Bells* –

> *The emptying train, wind in the ventilators,*
> *Puffs out to Egloskerry, to Tresmeer,*
> *Through minty meadows, under bearded trees*
> *And hills upon whose sides the clinging farms*
> *Hold Bible Christians . . . . .*

Now the North Cornwall branch of the London & South Western

Railways is no more, leaving only fast decaying sites for the industrial archaeologist to seek out, and the most visible record of the Bible Christians is the inscription on some Westcountry chapels – they amalgamated with the Methodists in 1907.

Like the Peculiar People in Essex at a later period, the Bible Christians were evangelists with no pretensions to be above their social class. Sylvester Horne says they took the name from their habit of carrying their Bibles under their arms, and says that the most 'adventurous and intrepid' missionaries of their cause were women. But at Shebbear in North Devon, where the sect originated, they had a boys' school and a printing press, and later they had a girls' school at Bideford. Writing in 1903, Horne was able to say that from the day they were founded, 'a month has not elapsed without a Bible Christian chapel being added to the total'. But this must be seen against the comment made by Jack Squire, a contributor to the present book, that some 'people of wider knowledge' were amused by the use of dialect – he quotes an example: 'They come yur hungry for the Word of the Lord and they went away starving' (starving here meaning ravenous – clearly the satisfaction of hunger had fed a new appetite).

Village life for chapel folk was not always easy, though the persecutions of two hundred years before would have been a folk memory by the nineteenth century. Contributors to this book speak of bigotry as late as the 1920s, but others record the village parson expecting a thin congregation when the Methodists were 'doing Messiah' (we shall return later to the musical traditions of the chapel). By the time of the First World War you could have found a range of chapels and chapel folk in the villages, which – at the risk of over-simplification – ran from the indigenous evangelical tabernacles, by way of the more 'respectable' denominations (Methodists of various persuasions, Baptists, Congregationalists, with here and there Presbyterians or Quakers) to the Anglican parish church itself, whose members and clergy must often have seen themselves as superior to the sects around them.

When we look at these distinctions through scholarly eyes we find them to have been duly classified. 'Churches', seen for example as the Anglican and Roman Catholic communions, are described as comprehensive, with 'a high degree of accommodation to the values and institutions of society at large' (to quote from the *Penguin Dictionary of Religions*). 'Sects', on the other hand, are taken to imply 'personal conversion as a condition of membership; and condemnation of the values and institutions of ordinary society'. In between we find 'denominations', which are 'more broadly

In Tillingham, one of Bensusan's villages in the Dengie Hundred of Essex, we have three traditions of village religion – the parish church, the Congregational chapel, and the meeting house of the Peculiar People.

based and open to ordinary society than sects, while less comprehensive and socially tolerant than churches'. In general, a connection is seen between the sects and the socially deprived, but it is also true that some of the denominations started life as sects.

Certainly these distinctions are complex, and in the villages of the period we are looking at, the social divisions would not usually have been rigid. Some farmers remained loyal to the chapels, and among those who worshipped regularly with the nonconformist denominations, just as those who attended the parish church, there would be men – rarely women – whose ·names were followed by the letters 'JP', or who were at the least parish councillors, and perhaps represented their divisions on the rural district or county council; even maybe the occasional alderman. Others no doubt were governors of the local elementary school, or even Guardians of the Poor. Tales are told of how the more crusty among their colleagues – establishment figures to a man or a woman – found it difficult to understand these people, with their radical views, who tended to speak up for the oppressed, and cared little about the protection of pheasant coverts. For them, as for the elder who preached to his flock three times each Sabbath in the richest local dialect, independence and the value of the individual soul mattered more than 'the station in life to which it has pleased God to call us'.

One thing that was most burdensome for dissenters in the villages was the invariable monopoly of the Church of England day-school. Under Balfour's Education Act of 1902 they even had to contribute, through the rates, to its upkeep, and this stuck in a lot of gullets. The Passive Resistance Movement that followed was led by Baptists, with Congregationalists supporting it; Wesleyans were less involved, and seem to have felt it misguided, but the resentment was strong enough to lead men to withhold payment. A few went to prison for conscience's sake, others, like the author's grandfather, had the bailiffs come in to seize their property – in his case, it was always the same barometer, which the local Citizen's Society duly bought back as soon as it came up for auction in the nearby town. Rural dissent could never live easily with the Tory Party.

For one thing, there remained in the nonconformist congregations well into the twentieth century a fear of Rome, and a suspicion of High-Church Anglican clergy. This was not altogether logical, and indeed the English Catholics, who have suffered as much persecution at the hands of the establishment as the dissenters have, might be said to have more in common with nonconformity than with the Church of England. But hear what Bensusan wrote, drawing from observation, about Ephraim the Carrier, who 'sets over' the chapel of the Peculiar People in Maychester, that rural metropolis of the Dengie Hundred, in the Essex marshlands.

Ephraim is relating to the man from Mudford how Mrs Mace, 'what was of th' Brethren and is now in glory' had been laid on her 'bed o'sickness', and was therefore unable to fulfil her offer to provide, for a small consideration, 'a meat puddin' an' also a apple pasty an' likewise a Christmas puddin' ' for the newly widowed preacher. It was then suggested that he be done the same service by Mrs Mace's daughter-in-law, at which point in the story Ephraim reports the full eloquence of his response –

> An' I no more to do but towd him to thank her kindly an' say I could manage. For that woman set under Reverend Spiller, what burnt incense an' encouraged 'bombinations an' believed in Transubstation, that false an' pornicious doctrine, an' would ha' bowed down to th' Pope if so be he'd come to Maychester, an' would ha' fallen down before him an' likewise worshipped him.

Those who wonder what the outcome of the Carrier's diatribe was must go to the original*, a book now sadly out of print. But the strength of his feelings and beliefs are here made plain, even though we are told in another story about the occasion when Reverend Blazer went on holiday, and Maychester went to the parish church *en masse* to hear a 'furriner' preach –

> Even the Dissenters, the Primitives, the Wesleyans, the Unitarians, the Methodists, the Peculiar People and representatives of other varied sects were present; having been loyal to their own in the morning or afternoon, they felt free to pay a rare visit to the beautiful old church with its pudding-stone walls, red-brick tower and gracious west doorway.

Perhaps in these two extracts we can hear the authentic voice of the countryside, with tolerance and bigotry side by side. The variety of dissenting experience shows through, and the social distinctions between the sects themselves were real, if pervious. But the difference between church and chapel is the central theme, and even where church is very much the weaker vessel, as in Wales and parts of the Westcountry, the reality of chapel remains. It is a religious thing – at worst, ranting preachers and intolerant congregations; at best a retention of very real and

---

* – *Comment from the Countryside*, by S L Bensusan. London: Noel Douglas, 1928.

fundamental doctrinal truths. It is compounded of revivalism, hymn-singing, Sunday School Anniversaries and Sunday School Treats. It has piety and pettiness within it. And if it is the religion of the underdog, it is also true that chapel folk have never felt themselves inferior. With all the social changes in rural society, it is alive and active today – and its roots go back into the origins of our political and religious freedom.

Professor Ferguson tells the story of a tiny station on the East Coast main line in Northumberland, Widdrington Halt, where on one occasion the Capitals Express (non-stop, Edinburgh to London) was brought to a stand by the signal. A first-class passenger leaned out of the train and asked the station-master cum ticket collector cum crossing keeper 'Is this King's Cross, my man?', to which the railwayman answered, in broad Geordie, 'Noa, but it's the same forrm.' Just so, comments the professor, the little Methodist cause where he heard the story belongs to the same firm as St Peter's, or St Paul's.

3

◊ Old Dissent ◊

IN the wooded country east of Chelmsford, the road slopes down from Danbury into the valley of the River Chelmer, through the village of Little Baddow. These are the 'Essex uplands', where farmers from the marshland went to find a wife – but the marshland farmers were known for remarrying, since their wives would not have the immunity to malaria, 'the ague' (pronounced a-gew), that was endemic on the lower lands. Essex is a county of fine churches, and plain chapels built of brick for nineteenth-century sects, with here and there a chapel whose congregation can look back much further into history than the time of the great revivals. Most of the buildings are younger by far, but it is not the bricks and mortar that counts, it is Hebrews Chapter 12, Verses 18 and 22: 'For you have not come to what may be touched . . . but you have come to Mount Zion and to the city of the living God, the heavenly Jerusalem . . .' It is the congregation singing Cowper's hymn, dating from the eighteenth century, and felt in their hearts today:

> Jesus, where'er The people meet,
> There they behold Thy mercy-seat:
> Where'er they seek Thee, Thou art found,
> And every place is hallowed ground

So the chapel at Little Baddow is not just the building. In the language of dissent, it is a 'cause', and its origins go back beyond Cowper's day to the previous century, while the building itself, unusually for a county chapel, dates from 1707. Let us look at its life over the years, and see how the strand of nonconformity may be unravelled from its first beginnings. For what today is Little Baddow United Reformed Church is not untypical of that strand.

In the seventeenth century the population here was about 250. It was in the diocese of London, and when Archbishop Laud made a visitation in 1637 its rector, a man called John Newton, was a friend of the puritan

Still in Tillingham, 'the beauty of holiness' and the plain beauty of the chapel.

divine, Thomas Hooker, who had been supported by the Corporation of the nearby town of Chelmsford to preach as a 'lecturer'. Laud put an end to this, but Newton enabled Hooker and his friend John Eliot to keep a school at Little Baddow, until government harassment drove them to emigrate, and Hooker became pastor of the First Church at Cambridge, Massachusetts, while Eliot achieved fame as a missionary to the Indians.

Hooker went on to found the State of Connecticut, and pilgrims from New England have returned over the years to maintain the link with Little Baddow. But the tradition of nonconformity remained in the village, and a generation later Thomas Gilson, the rector, who had been ordained as a Presbyterian, was ejected from the living in 1662, after the Restoration of the monarchy. Though he was unable to obtain a preacher's licence under the Declaration of Indulgence, another ejected minister, John Oakes of Boreham, did succeed, and he and those who followed him built up a congregation from among people of like mind in Little Baddow.

Continued repression made it impossible for the Presbyterian form of organisation to be practical, so the community of dissent came to take the form of the Congregational or Independent tradition. This was not unusual, and accounts for the relative rarity of early Presbyterian chapels, in contrast with those of Congregationalists and Baptists, but at Little Baddow there was a less common factor in support of the local cause.

In villages all over the country, the Restoration saw the parish churches return to the established church, with the active support of local squires, or even more distant patrons. But not all landowners were Erastians*, and at Little Baddow the Barrington family had a puritan tradition, and did not, like some, find it prudent to conform in 1660. Their support, in finance and in personal involvement, must have played a considerable part in the growing stability of the congregation. In her will Lady Barrington left funds 'for the better upholding and maintaining a preaching minister in the meeting house of Little Baddow', and her son Francis carried out her wishes, with the effect that a new meeting house – the one standing today – was built in 1707. His trustees were told that the aim of his family had been to provide resources for the congregation so that it might be 'exemplarily fruitful in piety and holiness toward God and in honesty and charity towards man'. Surely here we read the expression of aspirations that many unlettered members of the congregation would have felt, and that lie at the heart of the dissenting, evangelical traditions to this day.

The next Lord Barrington not only continued the financial support, but also attended service with his family in the chapel; this must have been unusual, but should be seen in the context of the relatively small number of dissenting chapels in that period, outwith the towns. Such support, though, we may assume, gave leadership and status to the congregation, which included ten people classified as 'gentlemen' and twenty-one who had the vote – fairly substantial numbers as a proportion of the small population, though it seems that many came from surrounding villages where no dissenting meetings were held.

The eighteenth century saw a pretty general weakening of dissent in England, and the cause at Little Baddow suffered a shock in 1758 when the second Lord Barrington decided to conform to the Church of England, and persuaded the minister of the chapel to accept the position of vicar of the parish. We can gain some insight into the minister's decision from the recorded observation that 'his character was not such as to produce any regret among his former friends that he had taken the step which he did'. But the spirit of dissent remained, though emigration reduced the number

---

* – Erastianism – The belief, named after Thomas Erastus (1524–83), that the State ought to have control over the Church even in ecclesiastical matters. (*Fontana Dictionary of Modern Thought*).

of members later in the century to five.

Even so, the chapel congregation continued to support a pastor, and even became involved in the affairs of the wider world. William Parry was minister from 1780 to 1799, and took an active part in the formation of the Essex Congregational Union, and in the foundation of the London Missionary Society. His successor, Stephen Morell, who came of a French Huguenot family, was minister for fifty-three years, and under him numbers recovered so much that the gallery had to be extended. This was a period when evangelism was spreading, and alongside the establishment of Methodism, which we shall come to in chapter five, other traditions of dissent were coming to be recognised as denominations.

But the mid-century saw a revival of zeal in the Church of England, not unconnected with Newman's departure to the Church of Rome, and Little Baddow felt the impact of this too. Despite Morell's attempts to help all in need 'uninfluenced by religious distinctions', he found that pressure upon the poor and those with small businesses to conform was so great as to amount to intimidation, with the implication that salvation was only to be found through the national church. In this he was certainly not alone, for the papers and reminiscences provided for the preparation of this book contained numerous examples of intolerance from all parts of England and Wales.

Despite this – or because of it – there were no fewer than ninety-four members who called Morell's son Thomas to succeed him in 1852. Ill health forced him to resign in 1877, and the cause then entered a period of decline in numbers, accounted for to some extent by the opening of independent chapels nearby, at Boreham and Danbury. But deeper changes were taking place, which were to alter the whole economic structure of the countryside, and to have lasting consequences for dissenting chapels everywhere.

In 1875 cheap grain from Canada and the USA flooded the English market, relieving the economy of the cities but destroying the home producers and ushering in the great agricultural depression. The wheat lands of Essex felt its impact more than some parts of the country, but everywhere there began the movement of population to the towns, only checked in more recent years by the purchase of rural cottages for retirement or second homes by town-dwellers.

Bankruptcies and unemployment continued until about 1899, when stock farming began to replace the arable, but by then there had been great changes at Little Baddow, reflecting a national upheaval. In 1877 a financial appeal raised funds for alterations to the chapel, but it was admitted that adversities had confronted the congregation following from 'the death of old friends, the agricultural depression, the migration from rural districts to the towns and the erection of neighbouring places of worship'.

Thirty years later, with the bicentenary of the chapel, the membership stood at thirty, despite the growing population of the parish, and it was described as consisting 'almost entirely of poor people' – who nevertheless succeeded in raising £240 to improve facilities for the Sunday School. There were 300 people at the dedicatory service, when the Revd C Silvester Horne MP (author of one of the sources for this book) preached on the text from Hebrews 12 that we read at the start of this chapter. Perhaps his choice of text reflects the faith of those who maintained the cause over so many years, seeing it as part of 'The general assembly and church of the firstborn, which are written in heaven . . .' The continuity of faith that we have seen in the story of this one village chapel is characteristic of 'old dissent'; the denominations that look back to the Reformation itself, and indeed beyond. They have in common a distrust of hierarchy, whether in church or state, and a profound belief in the sole validity of Scripture as

Set in the Wiltshire countryside, Horningsham Old Meeting – still in use for worship – is the oldest of our country chapels.

the source of faith and conduct. In this they look back to Wyclif and the Lollards of the fourteenth century, and with the suppression of Lollardry their history of persecution begins, as the state church seeks to maintain its power over the parishes, intolerant of both Protestant and Catholic recusancy.

The oldest chapel of all, at Horningsham in Wiltshire, not far from Longleat House, was built in 1566, with the permission of Sir John Thynne, who was at that time building the mansion. It was built so that some Scottish workman, employed by Sir John, could hold their own services according to the Presbyterian tradition. It seems that their isolation from like-minded communities brought about a gradual change to the Independent form of church government, so that the chapel, still in use today, came to be Congregationalist; and so it remains. (Many chapels that commenced in the Presbyterian form of government after 1662 eventually became Unitarian, but the Horningsham Old Meeting is an exception.)

Horningsham chapel is worth regarding as a place of pilgrimage, lying as it does in one of the loveliest villages of southern England. The thatched building set in the slope of the hill hardly seems ecclesiastical at all, but while its situation is impressive, it is the interior that will open your eyes to the continuity of chapel design, and the atmosphere of its worship. The high pulpit speaks of the place of preaching in the tradition of dissent, and it requires no great effort of imagination to feel for all the generations who have worshipped here, though sadly numbers are much reduced today. (The second oldest chapel, the Congregational building at Walpole, in Suffolk, seems to have been a casualty of rural depopulation, for it is no longer in use – in any event, though physically it may date from the sixteenth century, its use as a chapel dates, so it is stated, from 1647.)

The Horningsham congregation seems to have suffered very little in the days of bigotry and outright persecution, perhaps through the approval of the Thynne family at Longleat. In the eighteenth century there was some pressure to eject the minister, which the Earl of Weymouth would not allow; instead he confirmed the lease and gave a donation to the cause. In the present century the Marquess of Bath took a similarly generous interest. But in this it must be admitted that the Horningsham Old Meeting was fortunate – though its historian suggests that 'the little flock at the Old Meeting did not go seeking trouble', when bigotry became rampant after the Restoration.

The Conventicles Act of 1593 showed that tolerance was strained even under Queen Elizabeth, and the years of the Commonwealth were a period of peace and growth for many puritan congregations. But with the Act of Uniformity of 1662 dissent became illegal, and some 2,000 puritan and Presbyterian clergy were ejected from their livings, many of them going into extreme poverty for their faith. In 1664 the laity suffered too, when another Conventicles Act made it a punishable offence for more than five persons in addition to the members of a family to assemble for any religious purpose not in conformity with the Church of England. The Five Mile Act of 1667 forbade the ejected clergy from living within that distance of any town.

The martyrs of this period, such as Vavasour Powell, the Baptist

Dissenting chapels in the small towns and villages of Suffolk, dating from 1800 and earlier, and still in use in 1925.

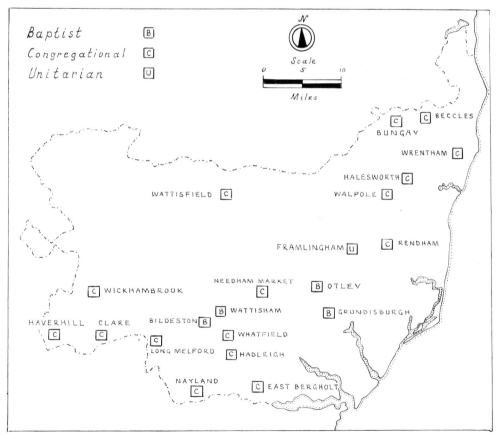

evangelist of Wales, and Colonel John Hutchinson, are little remembered today, but they were numerous, many of them dying in prison with no publicity to bring them to the public eye. In 1672 the Declaration of Indulgence gave a respite that was short-lived, to be followed by the atrocities of Judge Jeffreys and the Bloody Assize, directed primarily against the dissenters of the south-west. It was then that the last martyr was burned at Tyburn; Elizabeth Gaunt, a Baptist who had devoted herself to visiting criminals in prison – a kind of predecessor of Elizabeth Fry – but who was convicted of sheltering a fugitive.

The first flowering of dissent brought the formation of country chapels here and there after the Stuart tyranny had been ended in the Glorious Revolution – just three hundred years ago. But it was chiefly in the towns, among the industrialists and tradespeople, that it grew after 1688, and in the following century, when 'enthusiasm' became suspect and unfashionable, dissent came to require personal conviction, save where, in the great manufacturing cities that were growing up, it achieved a social respectability of its own. 'Rural dissent,' says Gay, 'was never widespread prior to the evangelical revival,' and this is born out in the map of Suffolk, the old heartland of nonconformity, where before 1800 there were no more than nineteen chapels in the villages and small towns.

With persecution a thing of the past there came a different threat, for there were still severe limitations to the civil rights of both Protestant and Catholic dissent. The universities were closed to all but Anglicans, and it was necessary to be a member of the established church to hold public office. The landed gentry and the better-off farmers, 'upwardly mobile' as we would say now, took to the parish church as a matter of course, leaving the Baptists and Congregationalists, more rarely the Presbyterians, here and there a Unitarian or Quaker community, to hold the loyalty of small groups of worshippers who, as the century passed, were (to quote Gay once more) 'fighting a losing battle against stagnation and decay'.

Sometimes we find the outcome to have been changes in denominational loyalty – as in the case of the High Chapel at Ravenstonedale, above Kirkby Stephen in Cumbria. Here the Presbyterian community established in 1662 became Independent in organisation in 1811, only to lose most of its members to a Wesleyan chapel built in 1839. Its recovery as a Congregational chapel followed, though, and one of its later ministers was the father of Bernard Lord Manning, perhaps the most distinguished layman that the denomination has ever known.

The story of Little Baddow, and these generalisations, are more than just historical reminiscence; they are the basis of a tradition that still forms part of the rural community's religious life. Little Baddow United Reformed Church today contributes to a witness whose boundaries are not those of the past, but it remains a cause whose life is consciously distinct. There is a sense in which the past is always with us, and for those denominations that look back to the seventeenth century for their earliest beginning, it is a long and eventful past. Contributions to the making of this book have included numerous studies of chapel history, each of them speaking of a need for people to know how they have come to be worshipping where they do, and – to return again to Hebrews, 12 – something about 'the spirits of just men made perfect'.

4

◦ The Life of the Chapel ◦

THE parish churches of many villages are buildings of great age, often of great beauty and impressive architecture, and they express the devotion of their founders and builders in past ages of great faith. They range from the magnificent; cathedrals in all but scale, like those at Cirencester and Lavenham; to the humble, almost domestic style of a thousand little-known but much loved places of worship. In many villages their doors stand open, and we can wander in, to look around, to wonder at all the stored history and devotion, and maybe to pray. We may have Pevsner in hand, to tell us about the architecture, or we may have Betjeman or Larkin in mind, with all they have to say about our heritage. Stand, now, for a moment in some village church, in whatever frame of mind you recall, and see in the mind's eye the chancel and the altar; feel the atmosphere of the place; observe the four or five other people looking round, and the two or three sitting or kneeling in the pews. Then leave by the great wooden door and the dark porch, as 'men turn from the providence of God into the warm sun'.

Would you expect all this from a visit to the chapel, half way down the village street?

But then, would you expect an exchange like this, that Charles Williams puts into his novel *The Place of the Lion*? We are outside a small, old, rather ugly Wesleyan church, on the façade of which its name appears in carved letters, Zion. At the end of the evening communion service – the breaking of bread – an elderly couple have come out of the chapel, to find a man behaving very strangely, and a younger man standing by.

> . . . The old gentleman stared, then he said to Richardson, in a voice not quite steady, 'Ill, is he?'
> 'O if he's ill,' the old lady said in a tone of pity. 'Would he like to come in and sit down for a few minutes? We live close by.'
> 'Yes, do,' the old gentleman added. 'A little rest – when my wife comes over faint – Well, Martha dear, you *do* sometimes come over faint.'
> 'There's ways of being bad besides coming over faint,' the old lady, now rather

pink, but still sweetly anxious to help, said, 'Do come in.'

'Thank you very much indeed,' Richardson said gravely, 'but I'm afraid it wouldn't help.' And then, by an irresistible impulse, 'I hope you had a happy service?'

They both looked at him with delight. 'Now that's very kind,' the old gentleman said. 'Thank you, sir, it was a very beautiful service.'

'Beautiful,' the old lady said. She hesitated, fumbling with her umbrella; then, taking sudden courage, she took a step towards Richardson and went on, 'You'll excuse me, sir, I know it's old-fashioned, and you quite a stranger, but – are you saved?'

Nonconformity, it may be, awaits its Betjeman or its Larkin, though it must be said that Pevsner awoke us to the value of its architecture, and maybe would not have accepted the use of the word 'ugly' in this passage. What it has got, though, is its own heritage of devotion, expressed, just like that of the great parish churches, in its chapels and meeting houses throughout the land. (But as to how Richardson answered, best turn to the novel to find out.)

For many people who know what it is like to stand in a village church, or even to go to a service there, the chapel will be unfamiliar – a strange, even slightly forbidding place, with iron railings before a gravel path, and like as not a large notice-board upon which there is fixed a poster with a text, describing itself as a 'Wayside Pulpit'. As to its interior, few but its members will have seen it, for it is likely to be locked for much of the time, and the doors open only to admit the faithful, for the Sunday or weeknight services, or the occasional funeral service. Could we but enter, and stand as we have been standing in the parish church, we would find a style and layout that reflects not just a different tradition but a deeper distinction that is a matter of doctrine.

To begin with, there will be no chancel, and no altar. Indeed, there will be no priestly function, and the communion table will have quite a different significance. A common element in the chapel worship is 'the priesthood of all believers', originating in the text from 2 Peter Chapter 2, Verse 9, 'But you are a chosen race, a royal priesthood, a holy nation, God's own people.' With this belief, it is no wonder that the congregation matters more than the building, and simplicity is all. The chapel community can often trace its origins to meetings held in the homes of the faithful, or in the open air, and the plainness of a room or even a barn is reflected in the architecture and interior design of the chapel itself.

Another reason for the simplicity of the chapel must be the lack of wealth of those who founded it, and who have continued its life. Some

Gressenhall Methodist Chapel, in Norfolk, worthy of its local name – *God's Cottage. (Mr Cyril Jolly)*

nonconformist churches in the towns and cities seem to reflect the material achievements of self-made men in the scale and even exuberance of their architecture, but in the villages this is hardly ever to be found. Yet there are chapels that date from the seventeenth century that can stand comparison with the finest architecture of their time, and there are plain, well-proportioned brick chapels from two hundred years later that are pleasing to look at, even if they make no such obvious claims upon our attention. And there are chapels being built today that show just as much care for 'plain good looks' as the best of those from the past.

But rather than dwelling upon the formal, and forbidding, aspect of the country chapel, let us look at some buildings that have retained the domestic style of their origins in the 'upper room'. For the first of these we go to the Norfolk village of Gressenhall, just outside East Dereham, where the Methodist chapel is known as 'God's Cottage'.

The building was once a barn, and the house to which it is attached may have been a farmhouse. It is not certain what denomination originally used it as a place of worship, but it seems likely that this use dates from the early nineteenth century, in view of the following certificate of authority, or licence, such as had been necessary since the Declaration of Indulgence of 1662:

> BE IT REMEMBERED that on the thirteenth day of July in the year of our Lord 1816, it was certified to the Lord Bishop of Norwich by ROBERT CHRISTMAS of the parish of Gressenhall in the county of Norfolk, farmer, by a written certificate under his hand bearing the date the eleventh day of the same Instant July (by exhibiting and bearing the same in the Registry Offices of the said Lord Bishop) that a certain building, newly erected and occupied as a School situated at the end of the street called Bittering Street, in the parish of Gressenhall in the county of Norfolk belonging to him, the said Robert Christmas, is intended forthwith as a place of religious worship by an assembly, a congregation of Protestants.
>
> Witness our hands CHAS. KITSON
> JOHN KITSON

Which congregation Robert Christmas intended should assemble in the building is unsure, but by 1827 the Primitive Methodists were holding a Sunday service at 2pm, and a Thursday evening preaching service. The Fakenham Circuit, to which it belonged, stretched twenty miles to the north to include the village chapel at Cley, on the Norfolk coast. In later years it was placed on several different circuits from time to time, and the cause may even have lapsed for a while; in 1835 there were fourteen members, and the Revd W G Bellham, as Superintendent of the Mattishall Circuit had to bring up four children on a stipend of £6.5s.4d a *quarter* – less than fifty pence a week in today's currency – which even so could not always be paid in full, a figure for 'back salary' being found in some circuit accounts that have survived.

The Gressenhall congregation belonged to several Methodist connexions until the 1932 amalgamation brought them into what is now the Methodist Church. In 1923 the building had been bought by the United Methodist Church, after a house-to-house collection had raised part of the money, and the owner had re-tiled the roof at his own expense. In Cyril Jolly's little book about God's Cottage there is a story of how a preacher from nearby North Elmham looked up from his sermon notes one warm summer afternoon to see three or four hens strut into the chapel. No one wanted to eject them, because of the commotion it might cause, so they were allowed to file with dignity to the front of the chapel, where 'after gazing about them and clucking in approval, they settled down until the service was over'.

There is a different feel to another of Cyril Jolly's records, in which he

God's creatures all

tells how the vicar on one occasion visited the chapel to speak to his head gardener, who was circuit steward at the time. 'Looking about him with unconcealed disdain [the vicar] said, "Freezer, I couldn't worship God in a barn!" The steward swiftly answered, "I could worship in a stable, sir, if the Lord was there!" ' But today the relationship between church and chapel at Gressenhall is a happy one, although in 1985 membership of the cause was down to ten. Even so, the doors remained open for those who wanted to worship there, and we may take our leave with the same words that Cyril Jolly ends his story, and that seem perfectly to fit these domestic walls, from William Cowper's hymn, the first verse of which we met in chapter three:

> *For Thou, within no walls confined,*
> *Inhabitest the humble mind:*
> *Such ever bring Thee where they come,*
> *And going, take Thee to their home.*

From Norfolk we turn to Cornwall, and to another domestic place of worship, resembling also a cottage: the Quaker meeting house at Kea, near

Truro, off the road to Falmouth, known as 'Come-to-Good'. Newly built in 1710, and opened on '13th of 6th month' (13th June), the name is a corruption of the Cornish Cwm-ty-coit, meaning the combe by the dwelling in the wood – but be that as it may, it is a name that bears a heartfelt message of welcome to the traveller.

Friends suffered severe persecution in Cornwall in the seventeenth century, and when George Fox visited the county to preach in 1656 he was imprisoned at Launceston in appalling conditions of filth. Yet from there he was able to write to Friends in the ministry, 'Be patterns, be examples in all countries, places, islands, nations, wherever you come; that your carriage and life may preach among all sorts of people, and to them. Then you will come to walk cheerfully over the world, answering that of God in every one; whereby in them ye may be a blessing, and make the witness of God in them to bless you.' Not alone in Quaker meeting houses, but in many chapels and for many years since, the message has been felt and understood, but there is no wonder that from such words there came to be so many Friends' meetings in Cornwall, one of them being Come-to-Good.

The domestic simplicity of the meeting house has been kept the same through various changes and extensions, with the thatched roof above it. Its doors, too, remain open for all who wish to worship there. Harry Pallett, who has written much about Come-to-Good, records that people from other denominations, especially Methodists, have joined Friends in their meetings, and one man he knew had actually been christened there – unusual, because the Quakers do not practise baptism. Here is the story as Harry Pallett recorded it:

> He explained that their chapel at Goon Piper was at that time closed for redecoration, so Friends at Come-to-Good, about a mile away, lent the Meeting House. 'Well, it so happened,' he continued, 'that my mother was a bit like that with my auntie' (indicating the situation with crossed fingers) 'or I could have been done there' (nodding across the road to the Carnon Downs Methodist Chapel). 'But me and Nellie . . . were christened in Come-to-Good Meeting House, so I tell everyone I'm half Quaker and half Methodist.'

If that story tells us something about chapel society, we can still turn to the beauty of the meeting house, little changed since L Violet Hodgkin described it in A Book of Quaker Saints, first published in 1917: 'The small old white meeting house is surrounded by a yet older small green burial ground, where long grasses, and flowers innumerable, cover the gentle

45

Chapels in country towns often have a style of their own – this is the Unitarian building at Bridport, in Dorset.

slopes. The soft mounds cluster round the walls; as if those who were laid there had wished that their bodies might rest as near as possible to the house of peace where their spirits had rested while on earth.' All the harshness sometimes associated with the practices of dissent have been lost here, and replaced by a spirit of devotion just as characteristic of the nonconformist tradition.

Yet while Come-to-Good has a long history of worship, for which purpose it was built, our third visit – to the North West – is to a chapel that, while domestic in style like God's Cottage, has been dedicated only since 1919, though the history of the worshipping community there is much longer. This is the Independent Methodist Church at High Legh, which is in Cheshire, close to the M56 motorway, and south-west of Warrington, by the main road to Knutsford. It was here, at the East Hall in 1813, that a young Scotsman called Robert Moffat took a job as head gardener, and the chapel still has the pulpit at which the young man preached who was later to extend the work of the London Missionary Society from South Africa into Rhodesia.

The Methodist meeting here began in 1783, when Betty Okell, who was thirty-nine and two years widowed, with seven children, opened her home for the purpose. But this in turn looked back to a meeting established some forty years previously, at Booth Bank in Millington. Wesley himself visited Booth Bank several times, sometimes preaching in the open air under a great oak, and sometimes in the home of Alice Cross, who, before her conversion by an itinerant Methodist preacher, had been notorious for her 'truculence and toughness of character'. Some part of that does not seem to have changed, as we see her through the eyes of John Pawson, another evangelist:

> She first began with her husband, who was a man of the same character as she had been. However, she was not to be hindered by him, do what he would. When it was time to go preaching, she would take her straw hat in one hand and hold the door by the other and would say in her plain way, with all possible seriousness, 'John Cross, wilt thou go to heaven with me? If thou wilt not, I am determined not to go to hell with thee.' He was prevailed to go along with her, was truly awakened, soon brought into the glorious liberty of the children of God and lived many years a uniform believer of the Lord Jesus Christ. They now gladly received the servants of God into their dwelling, had a pulpit fixed in their largest room, and had a church in their house for many years.

The meeting house interior in its original form, at *Come-to-Good* Friends' Meeting House, Gorran, Cornwall. (*Mr Robert Roskrow*)

High Legh Independent Methodist Chapel, in Cheshire, has the pulpit from which Robert Moffat, the missionary, first preached. (*Mr John A Dolan*)

Rural simplicity at High Legh, another chapel converted from secular uses. (*Mr John A Dolan*)

Such churches were not unusual in the area even before this, for Adam Martindale, who was ejected from the living of Rostherne in 1662, subsequently obtained a licence to preach in a house at Mere Heys. Martindale was a Presbyterian, but as well the Quakers established a meeting at Frandley in 1657, and a Baptist preacher called John Johnson was popular in the area in the 1750s. Between 1689 and 1735 there were eight houses in High Legh itself registered for worship by dissenting congregations.

Returning to Betty Okell and the meeting in her home, we must remember that Methodists did not at first regard themselves as a separate denomination, but as 'societies' with leadership exercised by 'class leaders', under the direction of 'round preachers' – the predecessors of the circuit plans of today. Services in Betty's home were held at 1.30pm on Sundays, so that people could also attend worship at Rostherne parish church.

Though Betty died in 1788, her family retained their loyalty and faith, and it was in the Okell home that the missionary, Robert Moffat, first preached. The community seems to have flourished, though the divisions within Methodism that took place in the nineteenth century lead to their transferring to the Independent Methodist Connexion in 1851, a change that was eased by the very fact that they possessed no chapel building. In 1873 the Okell family moved to a new farm, and with them went the High Legh Independent Methodist Church – and the much prized pulpit at which Robert Moffat had preached. By the end of the century there were Sunday services – known as 'the Okells' meeting' – in the afternoon and evening, and both preacher and congregation stayed for tea at the farm, with boiled eggs, bread and damson jam as the staple fare, and a special rocking-chair reserved for the preacher (which also still exists).

After the First World War many country estates were broken up, and at this time a good deal of land belonging to the East Hall Estate at High Legh came on to the market. One of the ministers on the Warrington Circuit, Robert Henshall, who owned a food preserving business in the town, bought a property known as 'Keeper's Cottage', with half an acre of land, opposite the Okells' farm. It cost £195.00, at which price he offered it to the church members, having estimated that they would need to raise a further £70.00 to convert the building for use as a chapel. The enthusiasm of the community was such that an appeal fund reached £188.12s.0d (£188.60) in just on a month. Work on converting the building progressed quickly, and it was opened on 10 April 1921.

Those who worship at High Legh, or those who go to find this country chapel in its apparent domesticity, must look back then on a history that is far older than the building itself in its present form and purpose. When the bicentenary was celebrated, in 1983, the speaker was Miss Eileen Tyson, the President of the Independent Methodist Connexion, and John Dolan, in his booklet *The Northwood Story*, records that she used a text (Hebrews Chapter 3, Verse 4) that seems to sum up the importance of the people for whom the chapel exists as a place of worship:

> For every house is built by some one, but the builder of all things is God (Revised Standard Version).

The same may be said of the next chapel, which is different in many ways, but with the same dedication in the making of it. The three we have looked at so far have all been ancient foundations, even if the building at High Legh is comparatively recent; at Tillingham, one of S L Bensusan's villages in the Dengie Hundred of Essex, there is a chapel that in some ways – to look at, at least – is more typical of its kind.

There are two, in fact, almost opposite each other. One is a meeting house of the Peculiar People, of whom there will be more to be said; for

In the United Church (United Reformed and Methodist) at Bridport, the nineteenth-century hammer-beam roof adds a touch of grandeur to chapel simplicity.

now, we turn to the Congregational church, opened in 1868. Thus it is a relative newcomer, but its origins are similar in some ways to those of Gressenhall and High Legh – a group of people, moved by their faith to form a congregation, and seeking a place of worship. Here, as in so many villages all over Britain, in the nineteenth century, they built new, and their building still stands.

In the middle of the century, preaching began in the neighbouring village of Steeple, initiated by a minister from the small town of Southminster, nearby. A chapel was opened at Steeple in 1857, and is still in use. Three years later the Steeple minister, the Revd G Seymour, visited Tillingham, 'and finding it scantily supplied with Gospel Preaching, he commenced preaching in the open air, where large congregations assembled.' At the end of the summer Mr Seymour moved his services into a barn, where he preached on Sunday afternoons and Tuesday evenings, and a Sunday School was started, which soon had seventy scholars. In the following August the barn was burnt down, and preaching returned to the open air, and then to a cottage in the winter, but by 1865 the cottage was no longer available, and the congregation decided to build a chapel of their own; this despite opposition, for there were by then several other places of worship in the village.

Despite this, the first brick was laid in August 1867, and the whole cost, apart from £8.00, had been raised by the day the chapel was first used for a service, on 28 January 1868. The cost had been made up as follows:

Land	£45.00
Building	£345.00
Interior	£45.00
Extras	£36.00
	£471.00

The life of the chapel after that was uneventful, in association with others in the Essex County Union of the Congregationalists. One unusual decision is recorded in the centenary leaflet – in 1914, 'To reduce the Church expenses, the trap which conveyed the Minister to Steeple on Sunday mornings, was dispensed with. The Church agreed, however, to provide tyres for the Minister's bicycle.' In 1968, when the Congregational and English Presbyterian Churches joined to form the United Reformed Church, the Tillingham community chose to withdraw and to continue as a Congregational church, in association with one of the new denominations that were established as a result of that union.

From the outside, the Tillingham chapel looks uninspiring when compared with the magnificence of the parish church on the square, further up the street. Like most village chapels, it is not likely to be open to the public unless a service is taking place, which means that its interior cannot readily be appreciated. Yet the proportions of the building, and the simplicity of its decoration and fittings cannot fail to impress the visitor. With a facade something more ecclesiastical than the plain box-like building of the Peculiars across the road; domestic in its use of the local brick; looking back to the great spread of nonconformity in the nineteenth century rather than to the founding fathers of the seventeenth, Tillingham Congregational Church can stand for the typical country chapel of today.

Not that all chapels are as formal as this – one Baptist chapel at Woodseats, outside Sheffield (and then a country village) was above a stable, and the horses stamping their hoofs could be heard during the service. At Thorpe Market, in Norfolk some ninety years ago the Methodist service was held in a large room in the house of one of their members, who had made forms and stools to sit on, and a pulpit. In the summer, camp meetings were held on the village green, and the story is told of one preacher who, being a very small man, was given an upturned barrel to stand on. He had just announced his text, John, Chapter 16, Verse 16: 'A little while, and ye shall not see me . . .', when the top of the barrel collapsed, and he himself was lost to sight.

For those who would like to see the interior of a chapel but who do not want to attend a service, it may be possible to arrange for the doors to be opened, by asking the church secretary, or the minister, whose names will be on the notice-board outside. But since these will be busy people, it would be as well to visit at a time convenient to them, and it is a necessary courtesy to ask permission before taking any photographs. With such an

approach, the experience may be quite as rewarding as a visit to the ancient parish church in the same village.

While some nonconformist churches in towns and cities have a pretentious atmosphere, reflecting perhaps the wealth of some Victorian manufacturers who endowed them, the village chapels (still calling themselves churches, if not meeting houses) have quite the opposite character. But look for the ornamentation that is to be found – the illuminated text on the wall that faces you as you sit in the simple pews; the balustrade surrounding the dais, or the railings of the steps to the pulpit. The communion table itself may be plain deal, but in another chapel it may be well-proportioned oak, carefully polished. You will rarely find that typical item of church furniture, a font, for christenings will be carried out (invariably as part of an ordinary Sunday service, before the whole congregation) with the aid of a small receptacle that can be placed on the table.

Music plays a great part in all nonconformist chapel services, and every sect has always produced its own hymns. Though unaccompanied singing is not unknown, the possession of some kind of instrument is an objective

53

'Plain good looks' at Steeple in Essex, where the chapel was built, like so many, to house a congregation that first worshipped in the open air.

to be worked for. Rarely there may be a musicians' gallery in a really old chapel, but almost always there will be something more, and that will be an organ, or at least a harmonium. In view of the gentility of the piano, it is surprising that the organ should have been preferred throughout the great days of the chapels, sometimes meaning that considerable sums had to be raised for the more substantial instruments, but equally it must have been true that people could be found who had the ability to play them. Today the electronic organ is making some progress as a replacement for the older instruments, and the harmonium, with its peculiar tonal quality, is becoming a rarity.

Chapels today are usually lit by electricity, which is the universal rural energy supply. But in some places in the past they have had gas lighting, and many people will recall the moments of silent prayer during the evening service, when one became aware of the soft background hissing of the lights. Few now could recall their predecessors, the candles placed in glass tubes mounted on brackets at the end of each pew, yet these are associated with a pleasant reminiscence concerning a rather penny-pinching sidesman of past days. It is told that he would walk down the aisle as the last hymn was being sung, blowing out alternate candles, and that on one such occasion he was heard to sing:

> *O for a thousand tongues to (puff)*
> *My great Redeemer's (puff)* . . .

5

⋄ Finding the Chapels ⋄

THE periods of English architecture that produced our great parish churches and cathedrals – Saxon, Norman, Early English, Decorated, Perpendicular – sometimes leave the feeling that nothing followed but the repetitive nineteenth-century Gothic Revival. It took the insight and persuasion of Nikolaus Pevsner, especially through the 46-volume *Buildings of England*, to make public taste aware of the riches of much chapel architecture, so that John Piper could say* 'I love chapels as features of the British Landscape'.

Even so, it is easier to recognise and admire the fifteenth-century parish church as you drive through a village that is unfamiliar to you than it is to notice the seventeenth-century Congregational chapel, or the nineteenth-century Methodist one. Of all the visitors who have been awed by Lavenham's superb wool church, how many have stopped to reflect on the classical facade of the chapel at the other end of the street? And how many of those who affect to despise the Victorian bethels have taken the trouble to absorb the character of buildings like the chapels at Pontesbury or Newton Burgoland? The Jerusalem Methodist Chapel at Bethesda, near Caernarvon, has an almost Palladian flavour, but all over Wales there are buildings dating from the evangelical revivals that show a 'plain' good taste', reflecting an age of faith at least as impressive as that of the medieval church-builders. (They are indeed so numerous, and in the present age so often superfluous, that it is becoming a real problem to know what to do with them.)

If this book makes you take a new interest in chapel architecture, you will find three broad divisions by period. First there are the buildings that date from the late sixteenth century – the earliest seems to be the Congregational chapel at Horningsham, in Wiltshire, where, as we saw in chapter three, worship has been continuous since 1566. It is another example of the domestic style, which after the Toleration Act of 1689

---

* – Foreword to *Chapels and Meeting Houses*, by Kenneth Lindley (John Baker, 1969).

began to give way to a more formal, though simple kind of architecture. Baptist, Unitarian and occasionally Presbyterian chapels were also built fairly widely all over England and Wales during the period of 'old dissent', though never becoming as numerous as those of the second period, which begins with the evangelical revival and the spread of Methodism, at the end of the eighteenth century.

The second period saw the age of 'chapel planting', and lasted throughout the nineteenth century, when chapels were generally more formal in their appearance, and materials varied from corrugated iron to the local brick or stone of the district. These are the buildings that it is so easy to dismiss as dull and commonplace, yet at their best they have a subdued ecclesiastical symmetry that can be pleasing, and the way in which they blend with the domestic and commercial architecture of their neighbouring properties can perhaps account for their neglect by the taste of a later age. But we should not forget that more elaborate buildings can be seen, such as the Presbyterian chapel at Marsh Green, near Edenbridge, in Kent, with its accompanying school.

It may seem unexpected to suggest that a third, contemporary period can be identified, but it is true that some excellent examples of plain, goodlooking architecture can be found, dating from the twentieth century.

Do not be misled by a simple exterior – this is in fact the parish church of Ampney St Mary in Gloucestershire, even if it might be mistaken for a country chapel.

By way of contrast with Ampney St Mary, the Congregational chapel at Pontesbury in Shropshire has the yews that might be more readily associated with the village church.

Some of these belong to the evangelical tradition, as at Stratford St Mary in Suffolk, while at Burford there is a Catholic chapel of classic simplicity, reminiscent in its way of an earlier period of dissent.

But if you set out to find buildings to study and admire, you should not expect to find them all in the village street, or even in a side street of some small market town. To see some of them, unless you are a devoted walker or cyclist, you will need a car, and you will certainly need an Ordnance Survey map. Not every neat cross on the map – church or chapel without tower or spire – will turn out to repay a visit; some may be parish churches of the Anglican tradition, well worth a visit for their own sake, but not what we are looking for; others may strike us, to be honest, as dull (though that may mean nothing to the congregation that worships there). Sometimes, though, we shall be rewarded by a real discovery, such as the chapel that lies in almost total isolation amid the whins and birch trees on Aldringham Common, near Leiston in Suffolk.

Drive, walk or cycle along the road from Aldringham village towards Thorpeness, and you will soon be out of sight of any kind of settlement.

Chapel-building still continues, and some good styles may be found – here are two, one an Evangelical chapel at Stratford-St-Mary in Suffolk, and the other a Roman Catholic building at Burford, Oxfordshire.

Lonely and remote, Providence Chapel at Aldringham in Suffolk has style – happily it is to re-open for worship, too.

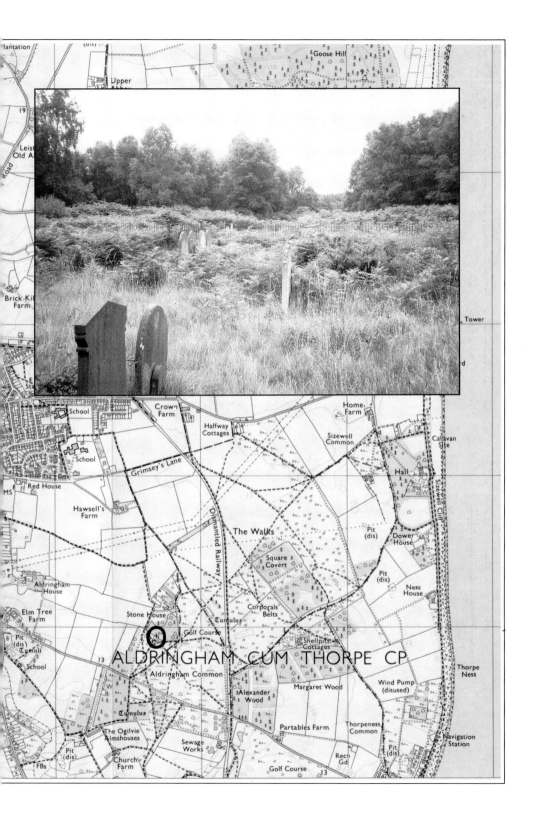

How should a chapel be found in such an empty place, you may ask. Watch out for a sign on your left, and turn up a track, where the whin bushes grow close and shelter you a little from the east wind, but before you reach the farm gate, turn right, and there before you, within its fence and graveyard, you will see a square, handsome building – not old, it is true, for it was erected in 1914, but of a style that gives grace to the wildness of the heath that surrounds it. No village; not even a handful of cottages; nothing but the open sky, and the trees and whins – and Providence Chapel.

A Strict Baptist congregation put up the original building, when they were given the land so as to to enable them to escape what can only be called persecution in their cottage meetings at Thorpe, and the hostility of many in Aldeburgh to the 'pograms', as the dissenters were called in Suffolk. Whether to get these difficult people out of the way, or for motives of gain, the land came from 'someone belonging to a family opposed to dissent', and it was offered with the proviso that the bricks for building a chapel should be bought from the vendor. About a year later, on 25 July 1812, the new chapel was opened.

Stand again at the door, and look around you. It is gathering dusk and there is rain in the air; the wind sighs and a few rooks fly homeward. Yet for 150 years people made their way to this place, for Sunday worship, and when the original building was found to be unsafe, the congregation set to and raised funds for a new one. At Easter 1914 it was announced that the plans of Mr Cecil Lay ARIBA had been accepted, that the work would cost £1,500 and that £900 had already been subscribed. Clearly this was no weak and struggling cause, as we can see from one of the tombstones: that of Eliza Markwell, who died 22 February 1914, aged 87 years – 'She was an Honoured Member of this Church for 60 years'.

Those who came each Sunday to Aldringham must have left some impact upon this place, for the atmosphere of it will move you if you have any imagination whatever. They came on foot or in farm carts, with perhaps a few of better means in some slightly more superior vehicles, and they came each Sunday, for the day. The practice of taking the family meal and spending the day at the chapel was common, and may not be unknown even now. On hot summer days, on this dry side of the country, or on days when the landscape would be hidden by snow and the east wind would bite through the light clothes of the poor, even their Sunday best; in all weathers they came here, and between the services there would be tea brewed, with each family contributing their quota of tea leaves to the urn.

Providence Chapel celebrated its 'ter-jubilee' at Easter 1962, but sadly

Surrounded by bracken, this tombstone at Aldringham
echoes the desolate surroundings in its inscription –

The rising morning can't assure
That we shall end the day:
For death stands ready at the door,
To take our lives away.

ceased to be used for worship in 1978. Yet its story is not ended, for it is to
be renovated and re-opened by an assembly of the Plymouth Brethren, and
people will still come to this lonely and lovely place to make their
devotions, in the peace of the Suffolk heathlands.

For very many chapels, though, the tide of faith has ebbed, to leave
them abandoned, with not even a notice-board outside to tell which
denomination it was that worshipped there. It is sad to think of the work
and loving care that has gone into such buildings, but the rural community
in which they flourished has changed beyond all expectation, with the
second agricultural revolution of the past fifty years. In Suffolk in 1925,

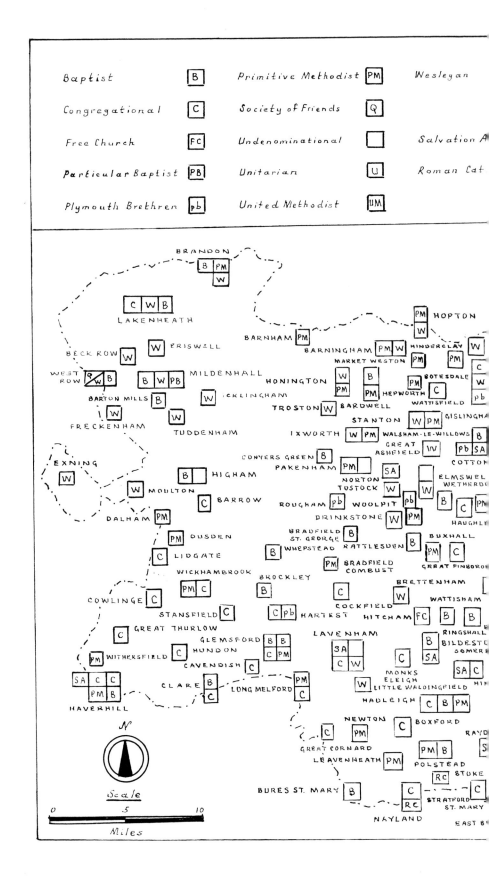

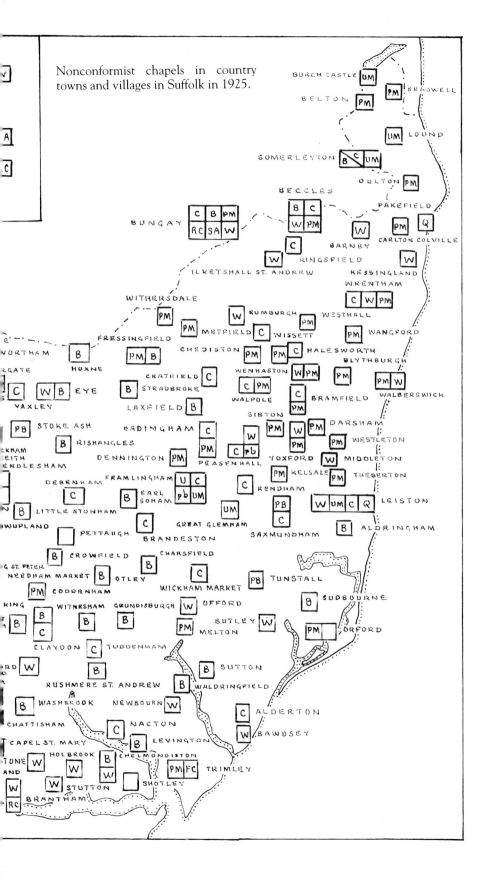

Nonconformist chapels in country towns and villages in Suffolk in 1925.

according to Kelly's directory, out of 481 parishes, 133 had a nonconformist chapel; 34 had 2; 9 had 3 and 8 had 4. In twelve parishes there were
two chapels of different Methodist persuasions, and in one there were
three, while there was one parish with two Baptist chapels, and one with
two belonging to the Congregationalists (the former at Mildenhall and the
latter at Haverhill). This list excludes the towns of Ipswich and Bury St
Edmunds, and the resort towns on the coast, so as to give a realistic picture
of the country chapel at perhaps its most prosperous period – it omits five
Roman Catholic and eight Salvation Army buildings that Kelly records as
well.

Yet this leaves 292 parishes, in this home of dissent, with no nonconformist chapel at all (in seven cases there seems to have been no church
either). And while nineteen Baptist or Congregational chapels date from
the period before 1800, the rest of them were founded in the 'chapel
planting' days that followed the great revival. Here is the distribution that
was to be found a generation ago in 'silly Suffolk' (the epithet is a distortion
of *seely*, meaning happy or blessed, and refers to an ancient reputation for
holiness, not foolish simplicity) –

Primitive Methodist	64
Congregational	58
Wesleyan	57
Baptist	52
Particular Baptist	12
United Methodist	8
Undenominational	6
Society of Friends	5
Free Church	3
Unitarian	1

Very many of these must have ceased to be used now, though some may
have been transferred to new denominational loyalties. So as you drive
through Suffolk – or any other county – you must not expect to find chapels
on every corner; it may take a sharp eye to spot the building, and closer
examination to tell what denomination it belongs to. Some of them are
limited to certain parts of the country, too; those of the Wesleyan Reform
Union being concentrated in the counties of the Peak District – South
Yorkshire, Notts and Derby, though at one time they had a chapel at
Penwith in Cornwall, which must have been the furthest to the west of any
chapel in England or Wales. Their territory does not overlap that of the
Independent Methodists, though; a denomination that has had some

distinguished lay members in recent years. In a letter, Christopher Monro points out that the geography of Independent Methodism is closely associated with the coal measures – here is his analysis of the location of their 112 chapels:

Wigan area of Greater Manchester			21 (1)
Remainder of Greater Manchester			19 (2)
Merseyside			11 (3)
Rest of old Lancashire			11
Warrington area (now Cheshire)			5
Adjoining counties:	West Yorkshire	6	
	Old Cheshire	2	
	Isle of Man	1	9
Further afield:	Staffordshire	3	
	Shropshire	1	
	Clwyd	1	5
North-east coast:			26 (4)
Others:	Loughborough	1	
	Bristol	4	5
Grand total			112

Notes: (1) The majority in a ten-mile radius of Wigan town centre
       (2) Including three each in Bolton and Oldham
       (3) None of these on the Wirral side of the water
       (4) Monro calls this 'the second heartland'

The association with coal provides an interesting possibility of research that Gay seems to have missed in his study of the geography of religion in England. So also does the sobriquet 'Quaker Methodists' or 'Singing Quakers', which seems to arise from the absence of any stipendiary ministers among the Independent Methodists.

Neither is there any infallible way of recognising a chapel by its architecture. While local materials were invariably used, there is a great difference between the uncompromising stone of a chapel in a northern mining village and the honey-coloured limestone of a small Cotswold town, where the ancient yews line the path to the chapel door. Some of these buildings are actually portable – Hervey Benham in his record of the Essex sailing barges* tells of an unusual freight; nothing less than the complete removal of a chapel from Colchester to Bursledon, 'pulpit and all; everything bar the parson', as the skipper put it. (The spritsail barges

---

* – Hervey Benham, *Down Tops'l* (Harrap, 2nd edn 1971).

frequently sailed with a whole stack on deck, so a chapel more or less made no difference.) This would have been a timber-framed building with wood or perhaps corrugated iron walls, and there is another story about such a chapel being moved across the street, when the minister insisted on travelling with it, actually standing in the pulpit, with his hat on.

It is when you get inside that you will really appreciate the nature of the chapel, for in most of them the interior can best be described as plain. Exceptions are the very early buildings, like the one at Walpole, near Halesworth in Suffolk, the second oldest in England, where the untreated wood of the furniture and a layout that resembles a Quaker meeting house rather than a nineteenth-century chapel provide a very special atmosphere. In some cases, on the other hand, the old pitchpine pews, with their sticky varnish, have been removed, and floors have even been carpeted, with chairs for the congregation to sit on.

Mostly, though, pews remain. Here and there they may have some style, as in the case of the box pews in the Congregational chapel at Cheadle, in

Staffordshire; in other cases they may be fairly basic, perhaps not much more than benches. In the very smallest chapels, you will come in through the door and find yourself in the aisle between two blocks of pews; a low platform facing you, with a table, a few chairs and a small pulpit; and perhaps a harmonium at the side. How far this must seem from the dignified proportions of the parish church, with its pillars and clerestory, its nave, screen and chancel! There may even be a bench below the platform, facing the pews, where those 'who are being saved' will be invited to sit, and perhaps to testify to their experience of salvation.

But you may not find it easy to gain entrance to a chapel of one of the evangelical sects, unless you attend a service, as Flora Poste does, in Stella Gibbons' novel, *Cold Comfort Farm*. The very intensity of religious experience in these chapels must provide its own atmosphere, every bit as impressive in its way as that of the great architecture of past centuries. We must not expect a great deal that is exceptional in the simple bethel, unless it is in the fire of the pastor's sermon, or the sincerity of 'the breaking of bread'.

Characteristic of the interior layout of almost every kind of non-conformist chapel, though, is the central position of the pulpit, usually placed high on the wall, facing the pews, and with the communion table

Rural depopulation has left the second oldest chapel, at Walpole, near Halesworth, in Suffolk, deserted in its homely style.

The communion table at Ridgewell Congregational Chapel in Essex, has a florid style quite unlike the usual provision. *(Pastor Frances Cleeves)*

A typical chapel grouping of pulpit, communion table and harmonium, at Longney, near Gloucester. *(Mr J H Mills)*

below and in front of it. This is no accident, but a symbolic difference from the Anglican tradition, where the pulpit is invariably to one side of the opening to the chancel, and where the minister goes into it just to preach the sermon. In the chapel, the minister will conduct the whole service from the pulpit, unless it is a communion service, when he will sit at the table with the deacons or elders, who will distribute the elements to the congregation, but the symbolism goes deeper than that. It has been well said that the announcement of the text of the sermon in a nonconformist service has the significance of the raising of the Host in a Catholic ritual – and as seen later, the 'teaching ministry' is central to the nonconformist tradition.

The communion table itself may well be very plain, but of good material and workmanship. It may have been presented to the chapel, like the one at Ridgewell in Essex (see page 70), which is reputed to have come from a Spanish wine-merchant's castle. The issue of whether there should be a table or an altar, so divisive during the English Reformation, is unequivocally settled here, so that the words of the prayer book 'We do not presume to come to this thy Table, O merciful Lord . . .' may echo in the minds of some who feel at home in both traditions.

For the ordinary morning and evening services, the dais on which the table stands may be used by the choir, giving rise to the lines in a spoof version of the song *The Village Blacksmith* –

> *He goes to church on Sundays*
> *The choir to admire.*

There may well be an organ, probably to one side of the building (leaving problems about what to do with the equivalent space on the other side). On the communion table there will be a vase of flowers, and the pulpit may have a reading desk built into it, over which an embroidered cloth may hang – very rarely with a cross, but perhaps with the letters IHS. The tradition of Protestant dissent has always distrusted iconography in even the simplest form, and the only example of religious art may be an illuminated text painted on the wall above the pulpit. Statues and sacred paintings are completely unacceptable, and for reasons of doctrine the crucifix is never to be found, being replaced by 'the empty Cross of the Resurrection'. Even so, in many chapels, and not least those in the villages, where tradition may be the stronger, the cross itself may be felt to carry Romish overtones, inappropriate to what is meant to be the 'upper room' of Scripture.

Pulpits, which seem such fixed and immovable objects, do at times migrate from one building to another. There is a nice irony about the Jacobean one in the United (URC and Methodist) chapel at Bridport, which has a date that appears to be 1659 on the front. It once stood in the parish church at Charmouth, where Bartholomew Wesley, great grand-father of John and Charles, was rector; he is said to have preached a sermon on one occasion for two hours (not unusual in those days), which gave Charles II time to make good his flight through the town. How strange that the good rector's pulpit should find its home today in a dissenting meeting house!

The body of the chapel will be taken up with the rows of pews, often set on a slightly raised floor of wood, and sometimes with cloth runners on the seats (which obviate that uncomfortable experience of sticking to the varnish on warm Sunday mornings). Hassocks are unknown, for prayer takes place with the people sitting or standing, never kneeling. At the end of a pew, at intervals along the aisle, there may be a cast-iron umbrella rack, with a kind of dish at its foot to catch the water, and these will be

Chapels have paths and gardens that must be kept tidy, too. This is the Baptist chapel at Lechlade, Gloucestershire.

worth examining, in case they may be individually designed, from a local foundry, though it is more likely that they will have come from a firm of ecclesiastical contractors. (Could there be a certain status associated with sitting in one of the rows with such a rack, denied to other, umbrella-less, members of the congregation?)

The aisle itself will be floored with tiles, but it may also have an iron grid running the length of it, containing the hot water pipe. It is a fortunate chapel in these days that can afford gas or oil central heating, and many an ancient and superannuated solid fuel stove has to do duty to try and take the chill off a chapel that is only used on Sundays. The grid can well be the scourge of anyone wearing high heels, though one suspects that an element of judgement may be discerned by older members when one of the young women in the choir finds her shoe caught firmly in this decorative feature of the floor.

At the back of the chapel (which, from the outside, is the front), there will in all but the simplest of buildings be the vestibule – a word that seems to have come down a long way from its Latin use for an entrance court. It will be formed by a wooden screen, perhaps with opaque glass panels, whose function is to keep the draught from the door or doors out of the body of the chapel, but in so doing it provides a circulating area where people can meet and chat, and to which the minister will proceed after the service, to shake hands with people and talk, much as the parish priest will be doing in the church porch. There will be notices here, too, and hymn books for the sidesmen to give out (prayer books, of course, being totally contrary to nonconformist tradition). What we shall not expect to find is any kind of cloakroom, for the heating – such as it is – means that people expect to keep their coats on (and the ladies their hats).

One thing that distinguishes the country chapel from its urban sisters is that it is more likely to have a graveyard, even if it is no longer in use. Often the older chapel buildings will have their surrounding trees, or even an avenue of yews, and there may be ornamental ironwork in the shape of gates and fences – they were usually spared when metal was requisitioned in the Second World War. Keeping the purlieus tidy is another responsibility – at Horningsham until 1964 the old graveyard was mown by hand – there is a photograph of the mowing team taken in June 1951, notable because it includes the minister, Revd A E Banton, and five of his deacons, among a total of seventeen good men and true.

It may still be possible to find a chapel with a coke-burning 'tortoise' stove, and it may also be that there is a clock. (If there is, you may expect

it to face the pulpit, its function being to tell the preacher the time, not the people who have to listen to his sermon!) Professor Ferguson tells the story of a chapel in Norfolk whose secretary 'liked to run the show'. A visiting preacher came one Sunday, and in the vestry, Bill, the Secretary, asked if the visitor wanted him to read the notices. 'O, don't bother, I'll do them,' was the reply, which was clearly *not* the right one.

Bill was restless during the service, and as the sermon began he was shifting uneasily in his seat, until his eye lighted upon the clock, and lit up. In the midst of the preacher's words he got up and fetched a chair, stood upon it, and turned a very noisy key, crunch – crunch – crunch. When it came to the evening service, with the same preacher, he could hardly find an excuse to wind the clock again, but, not to be outdone, he found it necessary to get up, open the tortoise stove with a clang, and tip coke into it, finally picking up the pieces he had spilt and putting them back individualy, plonk – plonk – plonk. So if you find a stove, or a big wall clock, remember Bill, for whom the chapel was more important than the preacher.

6

◆ The Minister in the Pulpit ◆

D R Nathaniel Micklem, in a little book published in 1943[*], describes a chapel as he recalled it from his childhood – 'it had been built . . . under the Five Mile Act, when our fathers suffered persecution, and John Milton had once worshipped there'. After a brief description of the building, he goes on to picture 'the congregation that has always gathered there'; it is the people that come from the surrounding settlements that matter, so much more than the bricks and mortar, and above all it is their reason for coming. Here, then is how he saw the congregation:

'Not many learned, not many rich, not many of great social standing have been amongst them. They have been sober, godly, country folk, whose religious convictions enabled them to brave, first, active persecution and, later, the disapproval and sometimes the covert mal-treatment of "the people who count", and, more particularly, of the parsons and the squires. Only men of strong character and personal religion would care to be associated with that congregation. The little Meeting House was their spiritual home, their refreshment and their joy. Their fellowship was based upon a solemn and explicit covenant with one another and with their Lord . . .

Their diet of worship was such as is unsuspected and unimagined within the gothic walls of the established church. For these simple people . . .'

> *their rough, home-brewed prayer*
> *To the State's mellower forms prefer.*

The prayers might lack something in elegance and classic form, but they were Biblical, passionate, direct and searching. All the life and experience, the joy and courage of the fellowship was expressed in the strong singing of the hymns . . .

---

[*] – *Congregationalism and the Church Catholic*, Independent Press. I am indebted to Mr N Micklem for permission to quote extensively from this source.

77

'After the solemn reading of God's Holy Word, after the fervent prayers and moving hymns there came the great moment, when the minister opened the Scriptures and declared once again the Gospel of the grace of God. Once a month the whole congregation met to solemnize the sacrament of the Table of the Lord, to break the bread and take the cup, and remember the Lord's death "till he come" . . . what a fellowship in the Gospel it was, what a communion in holy things!'

Admitting that this was to some extent an idealised picture, Dr Micklem claimed that 'on into the twentieth century' it was an ideal that could still be approached, as no doubt it can still be today. But for the understanding of 'chapel' it is good to turn to 'the great moment', the commencement of the sermon, round which the order of worship will turn. And it will do so whether the sermon is preached by an ordained minister or by a layman, for the congregation is gathered in order to hear the Word, and to *learn*. It seems this does not change – in a straw poll of pastors recently, including several from village churches, the importance of the sermon was invariably ranked highly, both by the pastors and by their flocks. What is still looked for is the 'teaching ministry'.

It is this that accounts for the central place of the pulpit, which we observed in the previous chapter. That position is clearly symbolic, speaking of the central place of the sermon. And it is this too that accounts for the educational requirements of the dissenting clergy, for if you will look at the notice-board outside the chapel, you may often find that the name of the minister is followed by academic qualifications.

The great 'preaching stations' in the cities that attracted the men whose sermons informed the nonconformist conscience have lost their standing now, but in their heyday they were matched in one way by the chapels of the villages and country towns; in the requirement that the minister should be an educated man. This in turn reflects the long years when dissenters were unable to attend the universities of Oxford or Cambridge, whose membership was limited to communicating members of the Church of England; they established their own academies, and at a time when scholarship in the ancient seats of learning was at a low ebb, contributed much to the intellectual life of the community. From them, and from the theological colleges (some of which remain) there came a stream of learning without which the British would have been the poorer, for so many of the great scholars of recent years have come from a nonconformist background, and often enough the chapel in the small country town.

But this contrast between the dissenting and the established churches must be modified to allow for the Methodist tradition, so strong in many villages, and not least in the chapels of Wales. Much of the early preaching of Wesley and his followers was in the open air, and for long the assumption was that the 'Societies' would consist of people who worshipped in their parish church, and held their own 'preaching service' at some other time on Sunday. Though Wesley never intended that his converts should leave the Church of England, in 1834 he was said to be 'like a strong and skilful rower [looking] one way while every stroke of the oar took him in the opposite direction'.

In the industrial towns and the Welsh mining valleys there was a growth of Methodism among people who were of no religious persuasion; in the villages and country towns the Methodists may have been nominal members of the state church, or they may have been attracted from the chapels of old dissent. Wherever they established themselves, though, they attracted to a greater or less degree the distaste of 'the people who count' for their evangelical fervour, and so they came inevitably, it seems now, to emerge as a denomination in their own right. (In view of their tendency to schism, perhaps one should say 'denominations'.) But it was in the villages as much as the cities that Wesley's influence was felt, so that

Part of a perfect row of Cotswold stone cottages, the Methodist chapel at Willersey in Gloucestershire makes itself known by its notice-board.

Gay can remark that 'Over large tracts of rural England Methodism has provided the only Nonconformist counterbalance to the Anglican Church.'

Yet Methodist worship, as Wesley provided for it, showed strong likenesses to the prayer book. The direction in which Wesley was in fact rowing, in addition to giving rise to a new denomination, brought Methodist worship closer to that of the other Free Churches, in which the whole service is felt to be a sacrament. And the importance of the ministry of the Word gave rise to the same demand for education in the Methodist chapels as had arisen among the Baptists and others before them. In many a country town or village, the Methodist minister, with his Free Church colleagues, has had a wider contribution to make to the life of the community than the requirements of his own flock would suggest; in many such places this is still true.

The social status of the chapel minister has never been very clear, and must have always depended to some extent upon the size of his congregation. But apart from the tendency for the nonconformists to expect better educational qualifications of their clergy than the Church of England did for so long, the chapel minister in a small country town could expect to be on a par with the bank manager and the doctor, and a step or two above the station-master (the latter depending upon the importance of the station). Whether walking or cycling, he would carry a certain air of authority as he went about on his visitations, carefully selecting the most suitable home to call upon at the right moment for afternoon tea. Neither was it unknown for the minister to become involved in local politics, even becoming chairman of the urban district council. Even in the villages, a settled pastor might similarly become a pillar of the local establishment.

But he might also be a thorn in the flesh of the establishment. It can never be possible to detach politics from religion – in many rural constituencies the Conservative Association is linked closely with the parish churches – and chapel has always tended to be 'agin the government'. For this example of how things could be in the pit villages I am indebted to Mrs Sadie K Ritchie, who sent me this extract from the diary of her father, a Methodist minister.

The date is Thursday 5 February 1925, and the place is the North Warwickshire Coalfield, on the outskirts of Nuneaton. The Arley Colliery Company, which had promised £50 a year for the local chapel, has notified the superintendent of the circuit that they would not give the money 'under existing conditions'. The diary continues:

I am the 'existing conditions'. What are we to make of a tit-bit of that sort in this the 20th century? I did not take my hat off when they sang the National Anthem at the Arley Memorial Service – Armistice Day – an action which seems to have caused a flutter in the Colliery camp. That is the charge. To put it bluntly, it is not a case of hats on or hats off, but because of my sympathies with the Labour Movement. It is nothing more nor less than persecution and victimisation. I can assure the Arley Colliery Co. that such methods will neither convert me nor help in modifying my political opinions, but rather the reverse.

As a matter of fact I have neither preached nor spoken in public on party politics since coming to Arley. I have often indulged in a friendly argument on social problems with the people here and there; a privilege which every man ought to enjoy without fear of the iron heel of the powers that be. Money? What will it not do! Remember Judas! He was not the last man to yield to the subtle temptation of gold.

The Lord have mercy on their miserable little souls.

There have always been exceptions, and they still exist. In many a quiet street in the small towns and villages of Britain you will find yet another tradition, and one that may even be flourishing more in the late twentieth century than everyone knows. History may even seem to be repeating itself, as the established church and the 'respectable' denominations tend to lose support, while the evangelical sects increase in strength and fervour. Sometimes they will have taken over redundant chapels from other congregations – surely a better use than conversion into a warehouse, or a second home; sometimes they have grown strong enough to build their own place of worship. Often, but not always, they will seek to avoid a 'high profile', resting upon the text in 2 Corinthians Chapter 6, Verse 17, 'Wherefore come out from among them, and be ye separate, saith the Lord . . .'

While the evangelical chapels may not set the same store on the formal education of their pastors, and, like other nonconformist denominations, may depend increasingly upon laymen in the pulpit, the central importance of 'the ministry of the Word and sacraments' that Dr Micklem described is equally valid for them. Preaching services, deriving from John Wesley's evangelism, and 'the breaking of bread' form the basis of their devotions – invariably announced with the proviso 'If the Lord wills'.

Neither is open-air preaching dead, though there is nothing now to compare with the Methodist 'camp meetings' of an earlier age. The 'Gospel Car', like the one illustrated on page 84, would act as both pulpit for the preacher and a stall for his evangelical literature, as well as

Knapton Methodist Chapel, near Malton, in Yorkshire, was originally a Quaker meeting house, while the building used now by Friends at Acomb, York, was a Methodist chapel until 1911. *(Mr P Thistlethwaite)*

providing him with living and sleeping quarters. This one was in use in the early years of the twentieth century, and the picture seems to have been taken in Teesdale; for local journeys it would have been drawn by two horses, provided by a local farmer, but for longer trips the car was 'trucked' – that is, sent by train. In the diary of the Methodist minister shown beside it we find the following entry:

> . . . Mr Stephenson removed the car from Hude Top to Station (sic) to be trucked for Tynemouth. We got the car safely on the truck and then it was too high for the gauge, which meant either a fresh truck or taking the wheels off the car to lower it . . . The Station-master decided to send for a more suitable truck.

Such were the problems of the evangelist – and of the railway servant! The minister, incidentally, seems to have had a way with railwaymen, for at one time he found himself booking a journey to Bishop's Castle, apparently on the railway of that name – he records 'I asked the porter if he thought I was luggage, when I saw the train, which consisted of 2 cattle trucks, 6 coal trucks and 2 carriages.'

Mr Jack Mills recalls from his childhood in the Gloucestershire village of Longney that there were in the 1920s two horse-drawn mission vans travelling through the area: 'The Caravan Mission to Village Children', and 'The Open Air Mission'. Normally the missioner would let down the flap of the van, and conduct the service from there, giving out tracts and leaflets from the store inside, but in bad weather he would have the local chapel available for his use.

Open-air evangelism continues today, one decidedly rural setting being the Royal Agricultural Society's Show at Stoneleigh Abbey, where the preachers have their own camp site, through the good offices of Lord Leigh, the owner of the estate. Gospel vans are used still, such as those of the Evangelical Movement of Wales, but they are Ford Transits, not horse-drawn affairs – yet the origins of the vans can be found in the eighteenth century. Many of today's travelling preachers, though, find themselves called to belong to no denomination, their account of their ordination being taken from John, Chapter 15, Verse 16: 'Ye have not chosen me, but I have chosen you, and ordained you, that ye should go and bring forth fruit, and that your fruit should remain . . .'

As we shall see in chapter eight, the pastor is called to the chapel, not directed to it by a higher level of authority – except for the Methodist Church, there *is* no higher authority in the world of nonconformity. And

The pit villages have their traditions, too – this would have been in the area of the Arley Colliery Company, which did not approve of a radical minister.

Ready for the road – vans like this were moved from place to place by goods train, as the mission programme proceeded. (*Mrs Sadie K Ritchie*) the pastor's place in 'opening the Scriptures and declaring the Gospel of the Grace of God' is not the sole preserve of an ordained ministry. While the Church of England has its Lay Readers, the ultimate responsibility lies with the parish priest; in the chapel the layman may speak from the pulpit with the voice of authority. A subtle distinction it might seem, but it can account for a kind of misunderstanding that is more likely to arise in a small rural community than in the impersonal world of the cities.

While old dissent began with an ordained ministry, of men who, in the earliest days, had been themselves ministers of the established church, from the eighteenth century revival on the chapels came to rely upon laymen in the ministry, and to organise their contribution. For the Methodists, and for many evangelical sects like them, this has meant the

Outdoor missions have not ceased. This one was taking place in Devon in about 1950. *(Mrs M Stevens)*

invention of the 'circuit', a word as redolent of Methodism as are those of Wesley's many great hymns. It is not surprising to find that circuits themselves have been seen as the unit of Methodist organisation, so that Cyril Jolly, whose book about God's Cottage at Gressenhall we looked at in chapter four, has also written about the circuit to which that chapel belongs*. The key to any circuit's life is its plan; a printed document that has been likened to Bradshaw's Railway Guide in both style and complexity, which shows where and when the ordained ministers and the laymen are to preach for a period of perhaps six months or a year. Circuit plans that survive from the past – they have become collectors' items in recent years – are often characteristic of the nineteenth-century jobbing printer, with his typeface and decorative borders that seem florid by today's standards of taste. The illustration shows a recent one, but the layout is unchanged from the past, with the names of the preachers listed against the names of

* – Cyril Jolly, *History of the East Dereham Methodist Circuit*. Geo. R Reeve, Wymondham, Norfolk, n.d., app. 1955. I am grateful to my colleague, Dr G Nelson, for drawing my attention to this impressive little book.

the chapels on the circuit. The key at the foot explains the various special occasions, one of them the daunting 'Tr. S' for Trial Sermon – an ordeal for a new preacher, publicly announced in advance! One thing that will be noticed is the small number of ordained ministers whose names appear on the plan.

This circuit plan is for the period 4 May to 31 August 1986, and forms part of a leaflet, with names and addresses of various officers, regulations for the chapels and the preachers to observe, and a letter from the circuit president. The principal officer of each chapel is its president, and only in one case is there listed a pastor instead. The circuit, with its own officers and committee, has become the ministry for these congregations, and a means for sharing the resources of the stronger ones with the weaker. Typically, it includes chapels in both towns and villages, a practice as common in the remoter parts of Norfolk as it is in this area of industrial towns and pit villages.

Still in Yorkshire, but looking back to 1842, in the endpapers of Kenneth Lindley's book *Chapels and Meeting Houses* you will find a memorable example, described in florid letters in its title as the Lord's Day Plan of the Wesleyan Methodist Preachers in the Wakefield Circuit. Here again the circuit contains many village causes, along with those of the larger towns, including three in Wakefield itself. In this plan, the preachers are listed at the side, and each has a number, which appears in the rows and columns of the plan to show where he is preaching on each Sunday. (The Wakefield churches at West Parade and Westgate-End had weeknight services as well, but many of the villages only ran to an evening service once every four weeks.) The proud possessor of this plan, a man 'On Trial', has marked his duties on it by neatly outlining the squares in which his number appears, and from this we see that he had only five Sundays in six months when he was not preaching at least once, usually in the smaller places. On Christmas Day 1842 we find him at Carr Gate for a service shown as taking place at $5\frac{1}{2}$ – the plan's shorthand for half past five in the evening. We may speculate as to how he found his way there. Incidentally, preachers who lived in the towns must always have had problems in visiting the village chapels. There are many stories of long distances covered on foot and by bicycle, but even in the heyday of the country bus, from 1945 to 1960, there were very few journeys on Sunday mornings, and even if there was the odd one, there was every likelihood that it went into the town from the villages.

Not that every visiting preacher was as welcome as the next. We hear

CHURCH	TIME	MAY 4	MAY 11	MAY 18	MAY 25	JUNE 1	JUNE 8	JUNE 15	JUNE 22
ROTHERHAM	6.15	B. Hyde	J.E. Nort-cliffe	S.P. C.P.	Miss J. Water-field	Mission Band	B.C. Ellison	S.P.	M.Mumfo Miss M. Vickers
MEXBOROUGH	2.30	W. Cutts	R.E.L. Hunt	S.P. C.P.	T. Yates	Miss E. Ward	J. Allport	Mrs. K. Barlow	Mrs. V. Steers
DALTON	6.00	Mission Band	B.C. Ellison	S.P.	J. Wadd-ington	S.P.	J.E. Nort-cliffe	S.P. C.P.	S.P. S.S.A.
ELSECAR	6.00	Mrs. P. Vardy	J. Griffiths	T. Yates	Rev.A. Hallidie Smith	T. Yates	Mrs. S. Allen S.S.A.	S.P. C.P.	B. Hyde
JUMP	11.15 6.00	Miss Haith-waite	J. Hunt	S.P. C.P.	Mission Band	S.P.	R.E.L. Hunt	Rev. D. Morris	Mrs. N. Jones
HOUGH LANE	10-45 6.00	B. Cocker S.S.A.	R. Thompson	Mrs. C. Boyle	J. Hunt J. Dent	T.R. Frost	W. Marsden	N. Ramsden	T. Wood
SWINTON	6.00	S.P.	S.P.	J. Turner	Mrs. Nickleson	J. Wadd-ington	P. Ibbot-son	Mrs. N. Palmer	G. Evans
WATH	11.00 6.00	B.C. Ellison	J.R. Evans	S.P. S.S.A.	R.E.L. Hunt	M.Mumford Miss Vickers	T. Yates	S.P. C.P.	S.P. J.Walte
MOUNT TABOR	3.00 6.00	S. Reed	Mrs. E. Winnard S.S.A.	S.P. Ms Haith-waite	S. France	S.P. W. Platts	Rev. F.C. Wilson	S.P. C.P.	Miss J. Land
HIGHTHORN	11.00 6.00	S.P.	S.P.	S.P.	S.P.	S.P.	S.P.	S.P.	S.P.
BOWBROOM	6.00	G. Evans	S.P. S.S.A.	S.P. C.P.	G.W. Badger	R.E.L. Hunt	B. Hyde	P. Beevers	Mrs. S. Warren F.S.
YORK ROAD	6.15	J.R. Evans	Mission Band	S.P. C.P.	N.G. Bromley	J. Allport	M. Trott	A. briggs	P. Ibbo son
WARMSWORTH	6.00	M. Mumford	S.P.	K. Thomas	S.P.	J. Hunt	S.P.	G. Britton	S.P.
ASKERN MISSION	3.00	S.P.	B. Hyde	B.C. Ellison	R.E.L. Hunt	K. Burton	J. Hunt	P. Burgoyne	S.P.

References
C.A. Chapel Anniversary
S.S.A. School Anniversary
C.E. Endeavour Services
C.S. Choir Anniversary
H.M.S. Home Mission Service

O.M.S. Overs
L.P.M.A. Lo Mutu
S.P. Supply
T.S. Tempe

The circuit plan

	6	13	20	27	3	10	17	24	31
			J U L Y				**A U G U S T**		
	S.P.	R. Evans	H. Sykes	Joint Service	S.P.	Joint Service	S.P.	Joint Service.	S.P.
rd	G. Tanser	N. Hamby	Mrs. E. Wilcock	T.R. Frost	J.E. Nort-cliffe	R.E.L. Hunt	J. Hunt	S.P.	G.H. Spencer
	S.P.	R.E.L. Hunt	J.R. Evans	S.P.	Joint Service	S.P.	Joint Service	S.P.	Joint Service
rd	J. Walters	T. Yates	P. Ibbut-son	R. Fingado	T. Yates	United Service	United Service	United Service	United Service
	M.Mumford Miss M.Vickers	A.H. Mann	B. Hyde Mrs. Barton	S.P.	S.P.	S.P.	S.P.	S.P.	S.P.
E. ck	R.E.L. Hunt	H. Veitch	J. Dunn Sp.S.	B.C. Ellison	T.R. Frost	Miss C. Beckett	J. Hunt	L. Hanks	G. Brooke
	S.P.	Mission Band	G. Tanser	J.E. Nort-cliffe	J.R. Evans	S.P.	H. Sykes	S.P.	R.E.L. Hunt
	S.P. J. Wadd-ington	Miss J. Water-field	B. Kay C.A.	B. Hyde	S.P.	J.E. Nort-cliffe	J.R. Evans	J. Griff-iths	Mission Band
	A. Grif-fiths	Miss M.Vickers A. Fisher	Miss E.A. Deighton	S.P. Miss Carr	H. Sykes	J. Grif-fiths	S.P. G. Con-nelly	K. Lodge	J.E. Nort-cliffe
	S.P.	S.P.	S.P.	S.P.	S.P.	S.P.	S.P.	S.P.	S.P.
B.	R. Evans	A. Johnson	Miss N. Pugh	S.P.	R. Fi--ado	W. Cutts	S.P.	J. Hunt	J. Allport
r	S. Taylor	B. Hyde	S.P.	M. Mumford	H. Sykes	S.P.	C. Jackson	Mr. & Mrs. Houghton	S.P.
y	S.P.	K. Thomas	S.P.	G. Britton	S.P.	G. Bailey	S.P.	K. Thomas	K. Thomas
on	M. Powler	J. Hunt	Miss M. Vickers	K. Burton	S.P.	B.C. Ellison	S.P.	J. Hunt	S.P.

P.A.	Primary Anniversary	S.	Lord's Supper
B.C.	Bible Class Services	H.	Hospital Sunday
F.S.	Flower Services	R.S.	Re-opening Services
W.A.	Women's Auxiliary Services	Sp.S	Special Service
O.S.	Ordination Service	Tr.S	Trial Sermon

of a representative from a village cause complaining about the sermons they had to endure under the local plan: 'Why shouldn't we 'ave a *good* man sometimes?' he said, with feeling; 'And why shouldn't them in Newbury see what the villages 'as to *contend* with?' Yet, to balance this, the same correspondent recalls her father being welcomed when he went to preach with the following unconscious humour: 'Oh, we do *thank* you for coming. Tidn't for what you puts in the plate; only you sez things so nice!'

One thing that stands out so clearly when these two circuit plans are compared is the importance today of women in the chapel ministry. Female evangelists were certainly not unknown in the revivalist days, as we saw in chapter four, in the story of Alice Cross at High Legh. While the more evangelical sects in the nineteenth century tended to segregate men and women in the chapels, and while the preaching was the responsibility of men, women expected to contribute to 'testimony', and their part was certainly not limited to the domestic requirements of the cause. No doubt the relative decline in church membership that has been felt throughout the twentieth century, combined with the loss of a generation of young men in the First World War, contributed to the growing acceptance of

Perhaps the strong sea air accounts for the rather florid touch in the design of this Methodist chapel at West Bay, Dorset.

women in the ministry, which the nonconformists never found much difficulty in accepting.

The collapse in agricultural employment over the past forty years may have had a further consequence in villages where chapel attendance has shrunk, for the few residents that have acquired and 'gentrified' the old cottages are unlikely to attend the local bethel. In some cases this has meant the virtual demise of a whole sect, as in the case of the Peculiar People, so often mentioned in Bensusan's stories of the Essex marshlands. But in many small towns and villages it is the ordained women in the pulpit that lead the worshipping community today.

How far, then, can Dr Micklem's ideal chapel experience be found today? If the key to it remains what he identified as the opening of the Scriptures, then the principle is unchanged. The country chapel, as we shall see in chapter ten, has always been a part of the social life of the community, but it is not and can never be just a kind of social club. It is a gathering for the ministry of the Word and sacraments, and the place of the pulpit is still central. If the falling numbers mean that there are fewer people training for the ministry, and fewer colleges for them to go to, yet the place of the lay ministry continues unchanged. In villages and country towns all over Britain, chapel remains a presence in society whose value only the future can judge.

7

◇ The People in the Pew ◇

THE nineteenth century knew that social class had a lot to do with where you went to church on Sunday. In one Essex country town, as late as the 1930s, your job could be at risk if you were not in the right pew – and, sad to say, 'chapel' employers were not above reproach in this respect. Where this was going on, it may well have sowed seeds of resentment, that contributed to the decline in attendance at both church and chapel after the Second World War. But the subtle correlation of faith and class was always a social reality, and so it remains.

It is very English, like that other nineteenth century distinction between, on the one hand, the London and North Western Railway and the Church of England, and, on the other, the Midland Railway and nonconformity. It shows itself, too, in the strength of Methodism in Wales, where the 'establishment' was English. Social class has been called 'the English disease', but the fact is that people like to know where they belong. Well may Kipling have said –

> For the Colonel's Lady an' Judy O'Grady
> Are sisters under their skins!

– but the Colonel's lady in any village, English or Welsh, would never have accepted it. In the village, people are expected to 'know their place', and not to take advantage, one way or the other.

But if in this chapter we examine the social aspect of the country chapels, let us not forget that the origins and the survival of them have always been primarily matters of faith. It was not class alone – or even principally – that led to the persecution of evangelical sects, as little as a century ago. In a period of drunkenness and foul language, those who set themselves apart could expect the resentment of people of their own class, whose lives were not above reproach – so it had been in the early days of Methodism, and so it was for the Brethren, the Society of Dependents, the Peculiar People, and other evangelical sects. For an example of what could happen, let us look at the kind of individuals who founded the sect that came to be called the Peculiar People, and that in 1956 became the Union of Evangelical Churches. Founded by James Banyard, at Rochford, in Essex, in 1837, the sect flourished despite, or perhaps because of a great deal of hostility.

Banyard himself was the son of a ploughman, and, like many another such evangelist, lived a rough and disreputable life for many years, though a clergyman said of him: 'Had he been an educated man there is reason to think that he would have occupied a good position in society'. When he was over thirty he became a reformed character, and joined the local Wesleyan chapel, but his real impact on society came after he experienced 'rebirth' in the London home of a Methodist preacher, William Bridges. He broke from the Methodists, though, preaching in homes and cottages and in the streets of Rochford and the villages of South Essex.

In a little over ten years the Banyardites had established chapels throughout the marshlands, and as far afield as Herongate and Witham; even in London there was one. In 1852 they decided to establish a church, taking their authority from the New Testament, with bishops, elders and assistants. The name they chose came from no fewer than four texts, including Deuteronomy 14, 2; Deuteronomy 26, 18–19; and Titus 2, 14; as well as the better-known one in 1 Peter 2, verse 9, which begins: 'But ye are a chosen generation, a royal priesthood, an holy nation, a peculiar people . . .' Their rapid growth was marked less by the hostility of the better-off, for South Essex had few big houses or estates, than by the violent attacks of their neighbours. At Great Wakering, it is recorded of Banyard that –

> A little man stood up to preach, and every time the door opened stones and brickbats were hurled in, but they never hit him, and the more they came the more the little man's eyes sparkled and shone.

Mark Sorrell, from whose book this memory is taken, tells us 'It was counted a sign that God was on their side, that the stones so frequently missed their target'.

The faith of the Peculiars was based upon the experience of rebirth, and they formed a close society, increasingly isolated from the people of the towns and villages where their chapels were to be found. But they gained respect, as hard-working and good-living communities so often do, and despite some tendency to fragmentation, survived to become a significant element in agricultural Essex, not least during the bad years of the great depression at the end of the nineteenth century. And though their sufferings at the hands of the establishment came to be severe, this did not involve any lack of respect for their faith, but rather the reverse.

From their beginnings the Peculiars believed in faith healing, and many examples of remarkable cures have been recorded. This, though, was to lead to their refusal to consult doctors, and in due course to their refusing treatment for their children for diphtheria and other contagious diseases, in defiance of the law. In the First World War, too, many of the young men sought registration as conscientious objectors, for the Council of the Peculiar People determined that 'War and Bloodshed is the work of Satan and absolutely contrary to the principles of the religion of Our Lord and Saviour Jesus Christ and the teaching of the New Testament'. In their insistence upon principle, in both of these areas of contention, many individual members suffered at the hands of the law, but they retained the respect of those who condemned them.

Such, then, is typically the faith of those who are called to the evangelical tradition, and if their attitude to desperately sick children seems hard to reconcile with it, let us remember that these children were nursed with loving care, in their own homes, and then let George Bernard Shaw have the last word:

> . . . no barrister, apparently, dreams of asking for the statistics of the relative case mortality in diphtheria among the Peculiars and among the believers in doctors, on which alone any valid opinion could be founded . . . the Peculiar goes unpitied to his cell, though nothing whatever has been proved except that his child died without the interference of a doctor as effectually as any of the hundreds of children who die every day of the same disease in the doctor's care. *

Now that the Essex Peculiars have transformed themselves into the Union of Evangelical Churches, they have identified themselves with a move-ment in the Christian Church that seems to have continuing strength, founded in the experience of personal conversion that was a factor in the spread of Methodism in years gone by. The same experience was central to another rural sect, established at Loxwood, in Sussex by John Sirgood in 1850; like Banyard of the Peculiar People, Sirgood was a disciple of William Bridges, a London hat-block maker, who had founded the Plumstead Peculiars in 1838. Sirgood's congregations came to be the Society of Dependents, and were concentrated in an area bounded by

---

* – Quoted by Mark Sorrell from the Preface to *The Doctor's Dilemma*.

Guildford, Horsham and Petworth – though, like the Essex sect, they had a few chapels elsewhere.

The Dependents had the same tradition of pacifism at the Banyardites, but they went further in rejecting the activities of the secular world, reading no published work save the Bible. A majority carried their beliefs to the extent of rejecting matrimony; not so as to permit promiscuity, but as a principle of celibacy, resting their argument in chapter seven of Paul's first Epistle to the Corinthians. We can see what they meant by reading verses 32 to 35 – 'the married man is anxious about worldly affairs, how to please his wife, and his interests are divided' (RSV), for example. (Whether St Paul was right to assume that the unmarried girl would be anxious about 'how to be holy in body and spirit' is a matter for textual exegesis that lies well beyond the purposes of this book.) In such a culture, it is hardly surprising that Dependency as a sect today 'is sustained only by the longevity of its members', as Dr Homan puts it. But it would be wrong to see them only as Montgomery caricatured them in that strange book *Abodes of Love**.

Despite persecution of the kind experienced by the Essex Peculiars, and later by the Salvation Army – on the part of the professional classes as well as the rougher element in rural society – the Dependents formed an active part of the community, owning many village stores, and even introducing the first taxi in Loxwood. The Brethren, on the other hand, who still flourish, have developed the principle of *separation* from the community (to be found in the early days of the Quakers, Baptists and Congregationalists) to the extent that they should separate *from evil*. This they carry to the extent of 'disfellowshipping' those who fail to meet their strict moral standards of behaviour; but it is important to recall their stress upon the family as the basis of their spiritual life. The maltreatment of children is unknown among the Brethren. Because they keep themselves separate in accordance with their principles, the presence of the Brethren may be little known in the wider community, but their high standards of probity in business matters must make a valuable contribution to the lives of their neighbours. They are not to be classified with the evangelical tradition that is still strong in many country chapels, but neither are they anything to do with the 'charismatic' movement; despite an occasional and unjustified bad press, they simply seek to practise a stricter code of morality than most of us would find comfortable, even though we could not but

---

* – John Montgomery, *Abodes of Love*, Putnam, 1962.

respect it. Though little known, they form an important denomination.

In the evangelical chapels, then, as well as in the longer-established churches of old dissent, great faith and spiritual strength has always gone along with a certain independence of mind that appears again and again in the story as a social, not just a religious awareness. If the squire worshipped in the parish church on Sundays, his labourers were at least free to attend their own place of worship on the Sabbath Day. There is a remarkable contrast here with the medieval world of sports and games in the churchyard, for the chapel tradition has always tended to distrust entertainments that were not of a directly religious or improving kind, and sports and games were seen as suitable only for children. Cyril Jolly tells that in 1874 the East Dereham Methodist Circuit decided to permit the Good Templars to use chapels and schoolrooms for entertainments, 'provided there are no personations or anything of a theatrical nature'. A programme of a more improving kind is illustrated on page 131.

The link between chapels and trade unions is well known, and the Agricultural Labourers' Union found that its members were often members too of one or another Methodist persuasion. In Dereham it seems to have been an embarrassment, for in 1873 the circuit resolved 'That the authorities of the Agricultural Labourers' Union be affectionately informed that it is illegal for them to hold their meetings in our chapels and they are hereby kindly requested to desist from holding them therein'. Behind the formality of the language, there seems to show itself a real concern, so that the words 'affectionately' and 'kindly' are *meant*. No doubt this reflected the employment of many of the members of the churches on the circuit, for only a generation ago, before the mechanisation of farming, the area organiser of the National Union of Agricultural Workers used to meet his members and collect their dues outside the Methodist chapels in the same part of Norfolk, after morning service.

That great nineteenth-century phenomenon, the nonconformist conscience, makes itself equally plain from the same source, with a resolution in 1890 congratulating Mr Gladstone on his attitude to the Parnell scandal – more than a hint here of an established puritanism, far removed from the insight of Yeats –

> And Parnell loved his country,
> And Parnell loved his lass.

There is more than a contrast of class here; rather a difference of culture, whose echoes are still with us. For the attitudes of the evangelical chapels were shared by the rather more middle-class members of older dissent, and virtues of thrift and temperance have never lost their significance. The Band of Hope encouraged children to sign the pledge (to abstain from alcohol), and few indeed were the chapel folk who had ever seen the inside of the village inn.

Always a few have moved in public life, sometimes people of some standing whose family traditions and beliefs have kept them faithful to the chapel; sometimes because their trade union and political activities have led them into office. Where a Tory establishment (sitting as independents) controlled a county or rural district council, a nonconformist farmer, committed to 'peace, retrenchment and reform' along with total abstinence and care for the poor, could be a great embarrassment. Such people, both men and women, fought to humanise the dreaded workhouses – in 1892 the Dereham Circuit expressed its thanks to a local MP, the Rt Hon R R Fowler, 'for his action in reducing the rateable qualification required for the office of Guardian of the Poor, thus enabling many who have hitherto been disqualified to occupy this position'. The resolution goes on to seek the abolition of plural voting and the introduction of the ballot, which shows us still more how the chapels kept the radical traditions alive.

'Villagers' and 'residents', then: the contrast was always a social one, and if in many villages there was only the parish church to attend on Sundays, in others, and in the country towns, there were growing alternatives throughout the nineteenth century and into the twentieth. And if in the chapels of old dissent the clergy were mainly middle class, in the evangelical sects, and this includes much of Methodism, the lay preachers came from the same section of the community as the faithful. The establishment might affect to look down upon them (and frequently actually did), but for their part, they were content to ignore such attitudes for the most part, or occasionally to make a reply that could be both telling and respectful. It has always been part of the tradition of the country chapel that it was for the 'likes of us' and not 'the likes of them'.

Nevertheless, the countryside does tend to be conservative in its social values, and the only evidence of a radical attitude amongst the reminiscences contributed to this book comes from the North of England, and the semi-industrialised villages of Yorkshire and Lancashire. In the south, it may be said, the command to preach the Gospel to all the world has – as it did in the nineteenth century – taken precedence over feeding the hungry nearer home. In the 1930s, fund-raising for the missionary society had a much higher profile than the needs of the hunger marchers, however much individual members of the chapels may have formed an exception.

The social standing of chapel folk has changed over the centuries, too. The meeting house at Ditchling, near Chichester, looks back to a congregation of General Baptists that emerged around 1645 as 'The Church of our Lord Jesus Christ meeting in and about Ditchelling' – a very good definition of the 'gathered church'. They worshipped in farm buildings until the chapel was built in or about 1741. We are told that 'among their members were families of substance, Yeoman farmers, Tradesmen and some humble folk. All were bound together by the practice of "Strict Communion" and extensive inter-marriage between the families'. By the end of the eighteenth century these people seem to have acquired a considerable status in the local community, and some of them were responsible for building the first village school in the years 1814–1834.

But thereafter 'the steam began to run out'. 'The children of the more prosperous no longer found membership of an unpopular organisation to their liking' – how often this must have been the case. 'Many of the less wealthy but equally able members emigrated to America and elsewhere.' Today the meeting house remains, but the social standing of its congregation is reflected by the 'remnant who hold things together', instead of the dominance of two hundred years ago.

For what has come to be called 'upward social mobility' has always been present to a certain extent. Later generations have not always wanted to follow the faith of their fathers, or mothers. Growing prosperity has sometimes meant growing conformity. And the social structure of rural Britain has changed beyond, it might seem, all recognition, for the working class is now in a minority there. In the final chapter we shall look at some of the consequences, but for the moment it is well to remember that 'chapel' offered generations of country people a niche in society that they could call their own, just as much as a framework for living out their faith.

That is why the significance of money appears in so many of the histories and reminiscences that have been used to make this book. For the chapel, its people would give their all – in the author's home town, the Primitive Methodists for long worshipped in 'the gooseberry chapel', so called because an old lady had raised so much by selling the produce of her garden, and giving the income to the cause. The average cost of building sixteen chapels in Norfolk between 1830 and 1892 was £218 each, and that included one extra-large building, the Primitive Methodist chapel at Dereham, which cost £1,030 in 1863.

Sometimes, as we have seen, land was given to build on; sometimes there were generous gifts towards construction and furnishing. Often a circuit or county union would have a fund for the assistance of smaller churches, and perhaps a national provision as well. But the independence of the chapel folk was expressed financially as well as socially, and through their own gifts, and their own hard work, they made the chapel their own. Anyone who knows village life will recognise the difference in attitude between the place where Lady Bountiful has presented the village hall and the one where local people have got together, raised the funds, and built it. It is in the latter place that you can expect the village hall to be an effective centre for the community.

And so it is for the chapel. Money, like all else, belongs to the Lord, and it is best put to the Lord's work. But it must be carefully used, and properly accounted for, and the accounting skills of a multitude of small business-men – bakers, shopkeepers, carriers – have been brought into service to keep the books. The young professional accountant of today ought not to despise the ability of the unlettered tradesmen, who gave such devotion to the work, and maintained the standards of the craft.

Sources of income have changed over the years. The biggest expenditure will always have been the minister's stipend, along with the provision of a manse, and after that the day-to-day outgoings would be mainly concerned with heating and lighting the chapel. Other expenses tended to arise on occasion, when for example it became necessary to spend on redecoration or repairs – the minutes of Horningsham Chapel have the following entry in the early years of this century:

> Resolved that funds be raised for thatching Chapel roof. The following were appointed to go round with collecting cards: Mr Charles Barker (Stalls district and around his home, beyond Scotland*); Miss Chapman and Miss Adlam (from the Batch as far as The Common and Scotland); Mr Moody (Pottle Street up to The Batch); Mr A Marsh and Mr Sydney Ford (Newbury to the Town well).

This effort raised £8.00, but Horningsham was fortunate in having such a generous neighbour, as we can see from a subsequent entry:

---

* – Scotland being a neighbourhood of the village.

Renovation. The Pastor had an interview with the Marquess of Bath . . . re present state of the Chapel and Burial Ground. After seeing for himself what needed to be done His Lordship very kindly offered to thatch the Chapel, to put in any new joists that might be required, and to beautify the inside walls at his own expense.

For many years there was a form of income that could cause considerable trouble, and that was found in the parish churches as well as the chapels: the pew rent. Sometime around 1860 we find the Horningsham Chapel discontinuing 'pew rents and quarterly collections', and introducing a weekly offering instead. We are so used to the idea of an offertory during each service that it may come as a surprise to find that pew rents survived well into the present century in many places – Horningsham may have been one of the pioneers of change. The problem was the element of property that went with the old system, which could cause a good deal of friction if a stranger was found sitting in a 'family pew', particularly where the family tended to make a stately entry half way through the singing of the first hymn. In any case, pew rents were a source of social divisiveness, for only the better-off could afford the commitment required. In that now all but forgotten story *Jessica's First Prayer**, there is a decent minister who goes in fear of snobbish pew-holders. But financial matters can always be a cause of embarrassment – in the author's childhood it was customary for the church secretary to go to the dais, just before the collection, to make the usual announcements, which always included the amount of money collected at the previous week's service. It may seem hard to reconcile this with the commandment that we should 'take no thought for the morrow', though there is virtue too in the proper keeping of accounts.

There was poverty, too, in the chapels. A Methodist minister's daughter recalls the Hemsworth Circuit in South Yorkshire in the depression years, where one family had only £2.15 a week *when the father was in work*, and could afford only a penny-halfpenny for the collection – a penny for the parent and a halfpenny for the child. Each Sunday they had to decide which parent and which child would go to chapel, rather than face the disgrace of putting nothing in the plate when it came round. Her mother's sewing and dressmaking was not just for the family, but almost literally in obedience to Matthew, Chapter 25, verse 36 – 'I was naked and ye clothed me'.

---

* – I am grateful to Christopher Monro for this reference. In a letter he says it is 'a well-written tale, much derided by those who possibly haven't read it' – though I've never derided it, I confess to being in the latter category.

Bowler hats and boaters at the stone-laying ceremony at Buckland Brewer, North Devon, in 1903 – the building was the Reed Memorial Chapel. *(Edith Brown)*

Indeed, a good deal of quiet social work has always been associated with the chapels. An example comes from the former Friends' meeting house at Witney, where in the 1930s a Women's Bright Hour was held on Wednesdays in the school room. The mothers sat on forms around a carpet on which their babies played with toys provided, and there was a short service, followed by a cup of tea, and time for a chat. But that was not all, for there were Thrift and Sick Clubs, with visits to any members who were ill, and there was also a choir, which competed in the local music festival. Very few of the mothers who attended were Friends, though some of them also went to the 'programmed mission meeting' on Sunday evenings.

In chapter ten we shall look at the social occasions; the fetes and sales-of-work and all the traditional ways of raising money. When the purpose was a new or refurbished building, enthusiasm and happiness marked all that was done – the jam-making, the sewing and knitting, the coaching of children to perform sketches of an improving nature. The congregation became a social group, linked by work as well as praise and prayer, in which everyone had a part to play, and was respected for it. Perhaps the lack of this bond in the latter part of our century, when chapel-building is rare, accounts to some extent for the decay in chapel attendance and life; there is not the same excitement in working for repairs to the roof, or a new central heating system, as there must have been for the visible construction of a new tabernacle.

As funds were accumulated, though, the work could commence. The footings in, there would be plans for the foundation stones to be laid, in a ceremony that would be duly reported by the local newspaper. For the curious today, there is a source of speculation as to who these worthies were, who a hundred years ago had the standing in the community such as to warrant their names being preserved by the stone-cutter. The president of the circuit and some local Justice of the Peace – perhaps a tradesman who had achieved public office along with his success, while remaining a chapel-goer in some neighbouring village or market-town. Did he perhaps make a special contribution to the funds, or was he a man whose faith commanded the respect of his fellow-worshippers? (Doubtless both would have been true.) Women are not infrequent in being commemorated thus, and maybe as many as four stones will be there, testifying to the significance of the new cause.

But then, as the walls rose, the pulpit and pews were delivered, and the glaziers and decorators got to work, the whole community could see the manifest achievement of the faithful, and there would be those to say 'It is the Lord's doing . . .' At last the great day would be able to be planned for, when the new chapel was to be 'opened' – the word consecrated would never be used, and services might well commence before the formal occasion. A weekday (or 'weeknight' if it was to be an evening event) would be usual, so that visitors from other chapels could attend and swell the throng without failing to be in their own pew on Sunday. An afternoon 'rally' and dedication might be followed by a more traditional evening service, with a sermon by the distinguished preacher who had been invited (never 'sent') to lead the formalities. More than likely, for the workers deserved their reward, there would be a meal of some sort, with trestle tables bearing cooked meat and tea. (According to season, this might be in the open air, or a convenient hall, or perhaps in what had been the meeting place for the congregation and was now to become the Sunday School.)

To raise and spend several hundred pounds in the nineteenth century, among a community of labourers and small tradespeople, was no mean achievement, even when we allow for the oversight of circuit or county union officials. The evidence shows that at times there were problems, but they seem rarely to have been burdensome, and many stories tell of faith rewarded with unexpected success. For the most part, though, what was needed was raised by the congregation, its members willingly and happily giving their small surplus, and working to make it grow and bear fruit.

The lay contribution, though, has always extended to the worship as well as the administration of the chapel. The Peculiar People, like many evangelical sects, spent a good deal of time in 'testimony', when the Brethren rehearsed the good things the Lord had done for them, to a supporting chorus of 'Hallelujah!', 'Praise the Lord!', or 'Glory!' And the tradition of the prayer meeting, often following a long service, is very old. There, the simple faith of chapel folk has its say, often very much in the vernacular – the author's father had a story about one old man, almost certainly unable to read, who made a pardonable mistake in the peroration of his prayer. 'Bring th' 'eathen to their knees, Lord,' he prayed, 'An' if their knees won't bend, ile 'em, Lord – ile 'em with th' ile o' Patmos.'

8

⋄ The Lay Responsibility ⋄

TRULY significant of the difference between 'church' and 'chapel' is the relationship between the clergy and the congregation. In Anglican terms, the parish priest is 'presented' to the living; the Roman Catholic hierarchy has its own method of appointing its priests. In contrast, the chapel congregation 'calls' a minister, having more or less freedom from superior authority in the process.

Calling a minister is clearly one of the most important functions of the chapel, and while it is the responsibility of the lay officers, it is unequivocally a spiritual function. Though all sorts of other things may disguise it, the process is governed by prayer, and, most remarkably, the assumption is that the 'call' must be felt by both minister and congregation to have spiritual authority. Even though, at the end of the process, the minister will be the paid servant of the congregation, his or her authority must be seen to rest upon some superior accreditation.

So let us join a not so untypical group of people in some village or country town, who worship together on Sundays, and work together for the survival of their cause. The minister who has served them for some years has made known that it is his intention to retire, first in private to the church secretary, the principal lay officer, and the deacons, but now formally, in the course of the morning service. The conversation in the vestibule as people are leaving can easily be imagined; mingled with regret and thanks as the minister moves among the departing congregation there will be an undertone of concern, even of a fear of the unknown. While there may be a well-defined process to arrive at the appointment of a new pastor, if anything goes wrong, they have no one to blame but themselves.

In many of the nonconformist churches, there will be someone to step in to help now. A neighbouring or a retired minister may be given 'oversight' during what is known as an interregnum, and will probably take the chair at the deacons' and church meetings, gathering the people with prayer as they face their testing time. Or the church secretary may be someone of standing, who can take the lead for the time being, supported by others who might be seen as 'elder statesmen'. One of their tasks, of course, will be to arrange for 'pulpit supply' after the incumbent has left the chapel, calling upon lay preachers and neighbouring ministers to take the Sunday services.

Where there is a circuit ministry, as in the Methodist tradition, this will be easier to arrange, and the officers of the circuit will play a larger part in the process of choice. But for our group, let us assume that the next step will be to notify the county or other area organisation of their position, and to make discreet enquiries about ministers who might be free to accept a call, including newly qualified students from the theological colleges. And now comes the most delicate part of the process, as the possibilities are discussed, and individuals invited to come and preach. At one time it was not unknown for a deputation to go and hear a potential minister preach at his own church, but if this sounds an embarrassment, think of such an expedition once headed by the author's grandfather, who lead the deacons in prayer *in the train*, on the way to morning service at a church in a nearby town.

So we must think of the deacons of the chapel, meeting to pray and to consider the progress of events. When it seems that someone might be suitable, there will usually be a report to church meeting, since that will be the body responsible eventually for the call. Then there may come the invitation to preach 'with a view to the pastorate', which is getting as close as one can to a decision, yet still falls short of it. For ultimately, the making and accepting of the call must carry with it the conviction, on the part of both the congregation and their new minister, that such is the wish of the Holy Spirit. What is in a sense a very human process is seen to carry a far superior accreditation.

The crowning event, then, after all this is done, will be a public act of worship, at which the new minister is inducted – and, if he or she is newly qualified, ordained as well. Such occasions are specially important for the congregation, and not least if it is a small country chapel, most of whose life is rarely open to such public recognition. In today's more tolerant atmosphere, it can be expected that the Anglican parish will be represented, perhaps with a prayer by the vicar; other nonconformist congregations will also be involved, with their clergy and members present or actually taking part. At the centre of such a service there are two formal acts, the giving of the charge to the minister and the charge to the church, which will be undertaken by people of standing in the denomination, and not

Renovation gave an opportunity for re-dedication here at Meshaw, near South Molton, Devon. (*Mrs M Stevens*)

necessarily clergy. In such ways do the chapels establish and re-establish the continuity of their congregational life.

But what we can see from this, and it is easily missed otherwise, is the responsibility of the layman. It is as old as English nonconformity, this notion that the authority in the chapel community lies in the voice of the Spirit, felt through church meeting, and active in every part of the life of the congregation, including the call to a new minister. And, as we have seen, this vision is possessed by a multitude of simple folk, and the responsibilities are discharged by men and women who may not be blessed by much education, nor able to lay claim to high social status. Certainly an active and enthusiastic minister may play a great part in the life and work of the chapel, but if he or she has wisdom and foresight, it will incorporate a care for bringing to fruition the abilities and confidence of the laity who will be the real bearers of its continuity in life and beliefs.

First amongst them there will generally be the church secretary and the treasurer. The main duties and certain legal responsibilities too will lie upon their shoulders. Alongside them we might expect to find the organist and the Sunday School superintendent, and of course, the caretaker. In a very small village chapel, several of these positions may well be held by the same person, but these are the essential lay responsibilities; and the only one that might be certain to receive an honorarium is the caretaker. If the numbers permit and require it, there may be other people with specific duties – perhaps a missionary secretary, or a youth organiser, but most of the other responsibilities, like running fetes and working parties, will be allocated on a one-off basis for each event.

The Sunday School movement was always a predominantly non-conformist affair, and very much a lay responsibility (though at times it might fall to the minister's wife to see to it). Early in the present century it was a major factor in the moral life of the nation, in town as well as country, and its decay seems to have set in most assuredly after 1945. But in 1911, for example, the Methodist Sunday School at Potter Hanworth in Lincolnshire had a membership of a hundred, in a parish whose population was only 454.

Methodism too had from John Wesley himself the tradition of the class meeting, where members were to tell of their recent experiences, and receive advice and encouragement from the class leader. Mr Tom Dewing recalls his first attendance, as a young member of the Primitive Methodist chapel at East Rudham, in Norfolk, early in this century: 'I was impressed,' he writes, 'by the testimony of a Mrs Huggins, a little woman who kept a sweet shop. "Well, friends," she said, "I'm glad I'm here. I'm glad I'm found in the place where His honour dwelleth; where He delights to meet with His needy creatures." Coming from the lips of an uneducated woman, that was rather striking.' Certainly it emphasises the contribution that the laity have always made to the worship and the spiritual life of the non-conformist churches – and not least in the village chapels.

One very necessary function, traditionally performed by laymen (and much more rarely by women), is that of the sidesman. Perhaps because of the element of ceremony involved, this tends to be a jealously guarded responsibility, to be discharged either by a regular sidesman for each aisle, or (if the numbers permit) on a rota. The sidesman must know where people expect to be able to occupy the same pew each week, so as not to embarrass anyone by putting strangers into it, and he will also have the function of handing out the hymn-books, and collecting them as the

107

congregation leaves. Woe betide the 'stand-in' on the occasion of the regular sidesman's holiday, if he makes his presence felt by error of any kind! (Most reprehensively by turning up late for his duties.)

Least known among the people who make chapel worship possible are the trustees. Since the building and the land are legal 'property', they must be owned by someone, yet while English law recognises a company of shareholders as a fictitious person, a company of worshippers does not have the same standing. But the law does recognise a trust, which may hold property and manage its finances. So it was not the congregation or the church officers that bought the land and paid for the chapel to be put up and furnished; it was this rather shadowy body of people who are its trustees. If there is a manse for the minister, they may own that too – they must do, if it is in freehold – and so they will have the final say in any changes or disposal of the property. In the more formally organised denominations there will usually be a central body of trustees, who will take responsibility for any chapel whose members may ask them to, but even so there will be many places where the chapel has its own local trust, managed by local people.

The lay responsibility means that someone has got to take a business-like approach to the work of the chapel, and in small towns and villages all over the country there are men and women who give their spare time to this kind of work, or who take it up on their retirement. Keeping the accounts, taking the minutes, dealing with formalities like the registration of weddings – it all involves much thought and care, and it is invariably a voluntary activity. Yet it is anything rather than a dry and tedious responsibility, for those who take on work like this will have a deep personal care for the cause they serve, and for them this, too, is much more than a secular task. In pastoral terms this is 'stewardship', but if the word is fairly new in this sense, the practice is as old as dissent, with its lack of endowments or wealthy patrons.

But although the members assembled in church meeting may not be anything more than an association or club in the eyes of the law, they see themselves as having the authority of Scripture to take their own decisions. On the one hand, these may concern the redecoration of the premises, and at the other extreme they may extend to matters of faith and church order; we have seen that from time to time they include the central decision as to calling a minister, and under the minister's guidance, they may deal with the order of worship and the choice of hymn-books. One of the things that distinguishes the denominations, though, is the extent to which the chapel community is an independent body of believers, and the contrasting element of control on the part of some superior association.

Many evangelical chapels cherish their autonomy – the Southern Baptists in the USA claim that there is no formal organisation above that level, although sociologists who have studied them say that something of the sort exists in practice. On the other hand, the Presbyterian Churches in England and Wales from the start retained the discipline of the synod. Methodism, as a pioneering movement with a strong evangelical flavour, developed the circuit so that the stronger chapels could help the weak, and some similar organisation is not uncommon in the small evangelical sects. Baptists and Congregationalists have retained the theological arguments for the independency of each congregation, but the nineteenth century saw the emergence of county, regional and national associations, or 'unions', which still never acquired a superior authority.

Belonging to such an association, with wider horizons, means a great deal to many of the chapel folk in the smaller places, who could otherwise feel cut off from the world. Delegates will be selected to attend the various committees, and in particular the annual assemblies – often held in late spring, and widely known as 'May Meetings'. This is very likely to be a lay function, and the delegates will be expected to report back to their own community when they return from the city where the assembly has been held, but for the people who go to these meetings, there is a reward in finding themselves among a multitude of others who share their faith and background that must be easier to imagine than it is to describe.

The life of the country chapel is linked in many ways like these with the communal life of the denomination to which it belongs. Some of its members, and many of the rural clergy, will be involved in the work of national and regional committees as well. Without this, it could be a lonely life for people with a small congregation, remote from the main centres of their faith.

But the daily, weekly and monthly life of the chapel still centre upon its own round of services and meetings. For the minister there are visits to be made, especially to sick and elderly members, and this piece of social work is an easily forgotten part of the job. Where there is trouble in a family it can easily become social work in the professional sense, but with a special quality of care. Now that hospitals are almost always in distant towns, the minister's visit may be a vital link with a patient's home; or the minister may be able to take relatives with him, where public transport makes visiting difficult – the National Health Service has not always concentrated its resources in ways that make it easy for people in the country to get to the local hospital, and demand is so erratic that bus services are not always justified – it is easy to neglect the minister's car as a vital element in the provision of rural transport.

Where preachers work on a circuit plan, the car is equally necessary, although in the past there has been many a long and arduous journey made by bicycle, and on foot as well, often in all kinds of weather. Many denominations have found it sensible to group rural churches so that one salaried minister has oversight of several causes, and this means travel too. But it is the weekly pattern of services that forms the central pivot of the life of minister and members alike.

An itinerant ministry also means that there is a need for hospitality. Nowadays the car may well permit the preacher to go home for a meal, so there is no longer the same significance in the chapel community that was expressed in the Edwardian parlour song 'When the Minister Comes to Tea'. But many a young student from college has had the unnerving experience of sitting at table with strangers – however kind and courteous they would be – to whom he would be preaching not long after the meal. Often there would be one member of the congregation who would have this responsibility, and whose children would have to be on their best behaviour; perhaps even a little overawed if it was a weighty figure from the circuit who sat down with them, and was respectfully invited to say grace.

The traditional pattern of Sunday morning and evening service, almost always at eleven and six o'clock, has been eroded in an age of declining membership, and often there is but one service in the village chapels that remain open today. Where there is a larger congregation, often in the country towns, the old pattern may remain, but the days of the 'thricers' – those who attended morning and evening service and taught in Sunday School in the afternoon – they have largely gone. But Sunday service remains the principal activity and purpose of the chapel, and the general meeting place for its members. Supplementing it there may be a prayer meeting on a weekday evening, or some kind of ladies' working party, preparing things for the next bazaar or sale of work, while the monthly routine will bring round the day of the communion service, invariably following morning or evening service on the first – sometimes also the third – Sunday in the month. Then, too, there will be minor patterns of life, such as the ladies' rota for the provision and arrangement of flowers for the communion table. This requires tact and understanding on the part of whoever is responsible for its organisation, in the same way as a rota for lighting the boiler in the absence of a permanent caretaker.

Added to this, there will be the 'meetings'. Church meeting, in many denominations, is the heart of the administration, although doctrinally it is not seen as a secular occasion, but as something with as much religious significance as Sunday services themselves. It will usually be a monthly event, and in the intervening period there will be a meeting of the deacons, or elders, elected by church meeting, and delegated with the detailed supervision of the spiritual as much as the administrative aspects of the life of the chapel. If the congregation is big enough, there may be other committees meeting too – for missionary activities, youth work, and so on, but in the small villages you may not find much activity of this kind. Where a larger church would have a premises committee or a finance committee, in the country chapel these would be the responsibility of the deacons.

Until perhaps a generation ago, the other main activity would have been the Sunday School. The future of any community is at risk, if it does not attract and retain the loyalty of each new generation, and from the evangelical revival on, the Sunday School movement provided for this. It may seem to have been essentially an urban phenomenon, catering for the poor and deprived, but it has been part of nonconformity in every aspect of its life. In many chapels today, children have their own 'junior church' to go to, after joining the adults for the first part of morning service, and the afternoon Sunday School tradition is less frequently to be found – some would say that it had the function of giving the parents a valued hour of privacy, which perhaps has been replaced by a Sunday afternoon shared by children and parents, often with an outing by car. Yet it is still a measure of the viability of the country chapel to look in the denominational Year Book, and see how many children are 'on the books'.

Along with Sunday School goes the teachers' meeting, and perhaps a training class for young people, led by the superintendent. There may also be a youth club, meeting on a week evening, to which the older children will graduate. Most of the denominations have some sort of national youth organisations, and there will be rallies, camping weekends and all sorts of activities intended to bring the young people forward to be the members and officers of the future. Fortunate is the country chapel that has the resources to develop work of this kind among its own congregation!

And then, of course, there will be the annual events. We shall be looking at treats and outings in chapter ten, and at that peculiarly non-conformist event, the anniversary, and we have already seen the importance of the annual meetings of the denomination. For the chapel itself, there will be one or two more occasions in the year, when the people will come together – an anthropologist might liken them to tribal gatherings. One will be the annual meeting of the church and congregation, when there will be formal reports and the presentation of accounts, but like most annual general meetings of voluntary associations, this may not be all that well attended! What the year turns upon, of course, must be the Feasts of the Church (though nonconformist tradition might not like the phrase) – and for the country chapel they will be Christmas, Eastertide, and, almost equally important – Harvest Festival. (Early nonconformity, and even contemporary evangelical persuasion, though, may unite in a distrust of Christmas, setting personal experience of conversion above any such doctrinal manifestation.)

Christmas and Easter are clearly the occasions when the minister is expected to lead the congregation in observing the central events of the Christian year. Harvest, on the other hand, is very much the layman's occasion. In urban congregations it may seem a formal recognition of some event that has become distant and irrelevant to the lives of the people, but in the country towns and villages it is still a real celebration, even though agriculture itself employs so many fewer people today than once it did. Gardens and allotments yield their produce; jam is made and flowers are gathered; a sheaf of corn may still be obtainable (though the modern harvesters will not produce it). Decorating the chapel for harvest is an event that brings together people who still have a real involvement in the produce of the land, and, what is more, a real feeling of gratitude as they sing 'Come, ye thankful people, come,' or 'We plough the fields, and scatter The good seed on the land'. And as they sing, their neighbours who attend the parish church will be engaged in harvest thanksgiving, too, for here we have a very human occasion that transcends denominational boundaries.

9

⋄ Sacred Music ⋄

D R R W Dale, the great nineteenth-century nonconformist preacher, once said 'Let me write the hymns of a church and I care not who writes the theology'. Much more recently, in the Clark Lectures of 1976*, Donald Davie showed the reality of a dissenting culture, and laid stress upon the poetry of hymns by Isaac Watts such as 'O God, our help in ages past', finding that Charles Wesley bears comparison with William Blake – consider, as a narrative poem, the words of the hymn 'Come, O Thou Traveller unknown'. The chapel hymn-book, symbolically handed to each arriving worshipper, is the receptacle of belief. Not that the hymn-book contains work solely by dissenting authors; think only of William Cowper and John Newton. Wesley himself was, with his brother, working within the framework of the Church of England. While some of the evangelical sects – such as the Peculiar People – produced their own hymn-books, as did the revivalists like Moody and Sankey, the majority of chapel-goers have been brought up on a selection of hymns that crosses all the denominational boundaries. At the same time, it speaks a lot for the place of the hymn-book, and for Dr Dale's remark, that the emerging sects should find it necessary to produce their own.

It must be admitted that many of the revivalist and sectarian hymns descend into doggerel, so that it may be hard to respect such lines as those beginning 'Here we suffer grief and pain, Over the road it is the same, And so it is next door', with their equally banal tune. Neither does the present age find much to commend it in the military language of 'Ho, my comrades, see the signal Waving from the sky' (though this does have a rather splendid tune). But it would be unpleasantly condescending to deny the sincerity of the uncultured hymn-writer, and the origins of the Peculiar People in the Essex field-workers are plain in this opening verse, quoted in Mark Sorrell's study of the sect –

---

* – Published as *A Gathered Church*, Routledge & Kegan Paul, 1978.

This is the field – the world below,
In which the sower came to sow;
Jesus the wheat – Satan the tares,
For so the Word of God declares.
And soon the reaping time will come,
And angels shout the harvest home.

There is a genuine voice here that sets to rights the jokey scene in the village chapel in Stella Gibbons' *Cold Comfort Farm*; and we must admit that weak rhymes and poor scansion (which do appear in later verses of this hymn) are not unknown in some contemporary effusions. Anyway, even Wordsworth ('Spade! with which Wilkinson hath tilled his lands') is not above reproach.

But if a hymn is – or should be – poetry, it is meant to be sung, and the music is, for the purposes of worship, as important as the words. Chapel has always been a place for singing, perhaps partly because of the minimum part played by ritual; at any rate, the fervour of chapel singing has often been contrasted with the reserve of an Anglican congregation. And while the Royal School of Church Music testifies to the place of music as an art in the cathedrals and parish churches, the place of congregational singing is associated more with the nonconformist churches. But yet, the professional organist, or church musician, of the larger urban chapels, with their robed choirs and weekly anthems, will not be found in the country chapel, unless by good fortune some retired musician is living in the district.

In practice, it may be surprising how often there is someone, though, who can 'play the organ for services'. And we have seen that the chapel invariably contains an instrument of some kind, so great is the importance of music. A faithful few may even maintain the contribution of the choir, though perhaps with no more than one or two voices for each of the four parts of the harmony. The people, not large in numbers but still in good voice, will continue to express their faith through the words of well-loved hymns, and to express at the same time their sense of being a community, a gathered church. Were he alive today, and present in a nonconformist chapel, Dr Dale would feel very much at home.

Hymns apart, though, there is a nonconformist musical tradition, choral rather than congregational, that lies mainly in the urban churches, where the annual oratorio has been and remains as significant a contribution to the music of the nation as the parish church or the cathedral. But the massed voices of Huddersfield, in whose performances Kathleen

Ferrier and many another international singer has been happy to join, are something far from the musical events of the country chapels – far in scale, and perhaps in artistic merit, though not so far in their occasion of devotion, and on the sheer enjoyment of the occasion by performers and audience alike.

Choir practice has long been another of the regular weekly events in the life of many chapels in the small country towns, and not only in the North of England either. Of the works performed, *Messiah* is the obvious standby, but Stainer's *Crucifixion* and other nineteenth-century works have retained their popularity where contemporary works have been adopted to a very limited extent. In one Yorkshire village we hear that the chapel choir 'augmented on special occasions by friends from other chapels' would not tackle only *Messiah* but Haydn's *Creation*, Mendelssohn's *Elijah*, and other works, and with well-known soloists. There is a deep suspicion in the culture of dissent of anything smacking of the theatre, or of 'art', unless the devotional element is very plain, and the natural conservatism of country people probably reinforces this. But the chapel that puts on a rendition of a sacred oratorio can expect an audience (and even a choir) that is reinforced from other congregations (including even the parish church) – there are stories of people slipping away early from evening service so as to hear the closing numbers of *Messiah* done at the Methodist chapel.

Where the choir has the capacity, the tradition of an anthem in the chapel service continues. The hymn-book may include a selection of pieces for the purpose, or there may be a well-thumbed set of anthems – even a more recent publication – that the organist can turn to in making a selection. We may speculate about the attitude of the congregation at this point; it is perhaps easier to enter into the mind of someone listening to a Scripture reading, to the sermon or the minister's extempore prayer, than it is to their reaction to choral music, whose words, if they can be deciphered, may well be entirely unfamiliar to them.

Still more unexpected may be the tradition, also still to be found in many places, of the solo. It is hard to imagine it happening in the atmosphere of evensong in the parish church, but *The Holy City*, sung by a soprano who has probably had some degree of voice training, can still be heard as part of the chapel service, the triumphal ending – 'Jerusalem! Jerusalem! lift up your gates and sing!' uplifting everyone's spirit too. What is much less often heard is the 'Women's Institute hymn', Blake's *Jerusalem*, so ironically chosen in view of Blake's identification of the 'dark satanic mills' with the churches!

115

But music requires some support. In the eighteenth century it was not only the churches that sometimes had musicians' galleries; some chapels did too, and someone who could play the fiddle or a wind instrument of some kind might be welcome to lead the singing. Instrumental skills must have been fairly common, for it seems that the singing in many chapels was supported in this way – perhaps by a cello and an oboe, or whatever combination was available. But the pipe organ is one of the oldest European musical instruments, and the spread of new churches and chapels in the nineteenth century went along with an accompaniment of organ-building. So the smallest country chapel might have an instrument, even if the poorest were provided with that strangely ecclesiastical device, the harmonium, and the violins and oboes of the past came to seem secular and out of place.

The harmonium depends upon the feet of the performer to work the bellows that gives life to its wheezy moaning, but the pipe organ requires those feet to be free to use the register of pedals along with the keyboard and the array of stops that confront anyone who sits down to play. Today the 'wind' is provided in most places by a small electric motor, but up to the middle of the present century it was a job that had to be done by hand. Somewhere at the side or the back of the organ there would be a wooden lever, and beside it a hard wooden bench, at which the organ-blower sat – usually, we may suppose, a boy, though the contributions to this book suggest that it was not unknown for a girl to have the job. Vigorous pumping would first be required to fill the bellows – a lead weight on a piece of string that passed over a pulley in sight of the blower indicated their state – and after that it was a matter of keeping them full; the process being repeated at the start of each hymn, as well as the opening and closing voluntaries, the music for the 'collection', and for any anthem or solo that was performed. Woe betide the organ blower who failed in that most vital – and least recognised – of the chapel's duties, so that the organ suddenly and embarrassingly died, waking some unfortunate lad from a moment's involuntary slumber. (Not, in the author's recollection, that it was easy to fall asleep on that very hard bench.)

For organ-blower and organist alike, the work could be demanding – not a little physical effort went into the performer's art, in the days before electric registers, to say nothing of the modern electronic instruments. This will be the background of the story told of a blind organist, who used to pin a notice in braille to the side of his bench, which he could read with his fingers, to remind him how many verses there were for each hymn – he

Modern style in a traditional building. Inside the United Church at Bridport, Dorset.

would find there the opening and closing lines, as well. We may sympathise with his feelings on the occasion when he found there, appropriately, 'Art thou weary, art thou languid – seven verses – Answer, Yes!'

An unusual example of 'industrial action' comes from the former Congregational chapel at Bridport, where in 1862 Stephen Champ, the

117

organist, was so dissatisfied with the organ that he insisted on the purchase of a new one, if he should stay. (The newly built church had acquired a 'poor little organ' from an earlier chapel building.) The result was a substantial instrument, built by John Walker of London, which is still in use.

In another way, the importance of the chapel hymns should not be forgotten. For agricultural workers and their children, education came late if at all before the reforms of the nineteenth century, and even after that, it gained support from the chapel that is easily forgotten today. As printed hymn-books became more common, so did the skill of reading begin to spread, as familiar words were seen to be associated with the pages of the book. For adults as well as children, this must have been a real contribution to the growth of literacy, and who can say it does not play its part in helping children to learn to read today?

At intervals in the making of this book it has seemed appropriate to use lines or verses from a variety of hymns. The way they are part of religious experience shows us the importance of music, in church and chapel alike, just as the popularity of *Songs of Praise* does on TV. There is no doubt that people enjoy singing hymns, especially old favourites, and one of the things that must stay with us in our thoughts of the country chapel is the sound of voices raised in quite uninhibited joy, as we pass the open doors on a summer Sunday. Better still is the blessing of being one of that congregation, engaged in such single-minded praise.

And what then of the same thing outdoors? Here is a record of the camp meeting at Hope's Gate Primitive Methodist Chapel, on the Minsterley Circuit in Shropshire, early this century, in the words of someone who took part in it each year, on the first Sunday in July –

> . . . four or five preachers were there; the senior preacher took the lead, and the others worked under him. This drew a large company of people from all round the circuit, although several other chapels held a Camp Meeting. The regular chapel-goers met outside the Chapel, and marched up to the top of the hill, 'very steep', singing hymns all the way. At the top they were joined by many more, and proceeded to a field, lent by a local farmer, where a farm dray was waiting, from which the speakers delivered their sermons. There was a board all round the dray, so they could all sit on the waggon, awaiting their turn, and the singing on a clear day could be heard for miles around.

118

10

◦ Treats, Outings and Festivals ◦

I T is late July in a small English town, in one of those inter-war summers
when the sun seems to have shone continuously. For twenty or thirty
children the great day has arrived – the Sunday School Treat. Last year
they had gone by hired coach to Clacton, but this time there is to be a
special carriage on the train, to take them to Walton-on-the-Naze.

Do not think of this as a 'poor children's outing', for at least half the boys
and girls come from middle-class homes, and for the rest, their parents
have taught them that they are as good as the others, partly because they
have sent them to Sunday School every Sunday afternoon since they were
old enough to go. Anyway, among the children themselves there is no
awareness of class distinction, whatever their parents may feel – from
middle through lower middle to working class, nonconformity has been a
great leveller, because it has put worship before class warfare. So the treat
is, for these children and their teachers, just another of the annually
repeated events of their experience of the chapel.

Nevertheless it is from all parts of the town that they come, from
cottages in mean streets and from detached houses in the 'better parts',
each with a packet of sandwiches and a few coppers to spend. (Here, too,
the levelling has been at work, for Veblen's notion of conspicuous
consumption has been modified by a feeling that too much spending is not
good for the soul.) There is no great distinction in dress, either – shorts for
the boys, cotton dresses for the girls, sandals that were as common then as
trainers are today; the penny-pinching that some of their parents have had
to practice to see that their children are nicely dressed is not apparent here
(although the teachers, coming from the middle class in most cases, may
be well aware of it).

Some of the younger ones, from 'the primary', will have their mothers
with them, ready to help the teachers with the supervision of the party.
After all, the special rates charged by the London & North Eastern
Railway make it a bit of a bargain for them too. The station-master appears
on the platform as the party gathers, and watches the teachers collecting

their classes around them, and making sure that everyone is there. The Sunday School superintendent and the Sunday School secretary, who have had the business of organising the whole thing, understandably leave the detailed responsibility to their colleagues, most of whom are female, and some young enough to have been Sunday School pupils not many years before.

In due course the train leaves, the station-master having made sure that all the party have joined the coach reserved for them, which is to be shunted onto a second train in the course of the journey. The peculiar dusty smell of a railway compartment on a hot day, the good behaviour of the children, under the watchful eyes of teachers and parents; the ripening harvest in such of the fields as are still under corn; all this leads to the arrival at the station at Walton, and the walk to the beach. (Once it might have been a procession, a witness, but this is the period of the 1930s, and of Free Church decline, and witness has gone out of fashion, at least in the south.) Games on the sand; a picnic, with tea from the thermoses that have been brought; some mild skylarking, and then the train journey home: not a lot has, it seems, actually *happened*, yet, fifty years later, that day is even now far from forgotten by those of us who were there.

Thus recalled, the Sunday School Treat is neither the evangelical experience, with hymn-singing and the like, nor the charitable event designed for the children of the urban slums that it will have been elsewhere, but it is probably nearer to the tradition of nonconformity in the countryside. A generation before, in the same small town, the only difference would have been in the distance travelled; then it had been a trip by farm waggon, the destination a disused and grass-grown gravel pit about a mile away on the 'back roads', where the same pattern of games and picnic took place. (Page 121 shows, surprisingly, how this could still be the form as late as the 1920s.) One contribution to this book recalls an outing like this, by canal barge (this was in Shropshire); another the habit in a Devon village of the different denominations organising a united outing to the seaside for the children in their various Sunday Schools. In yet another example, the children formed a procession through the village 'with banner waving and singing at strategic points'. There was a free tea, a packet of sweets and an orange, with races and games and the 'slunging' (scattering) of nuts by the Sunday School superintendent.

Processions of witness, on the other hand, such as the Whit Walks that, in their heyday, brought thousands of children on to the streets of northern cities, have never been so common in the villages, though they have not

Sunday School Treat as it used to be – at Jacobstow, North Cornwall. The unexpected thing is the late date: the card is captioned *Eden Chapel outing to Widemouth, Aug. 18th 1920*. Charabancs were about to replace the farm waggons by then. *(Mrs M Stevens)*

been unknown. In the south they might perhaps be felt as something of an eccentricity. For years, too, the nearest seaside was the great attraction, made possible for many country places by the development of motor transport – first the charabanc, then the 'all-weather saloon', and eventually, just the motor coach. But Sunday School attendance had started to fall by 1939, and has continued to do so, and today's outing is more likely to be for junior church – and to be a trip to the nearest theme park. Thus the distinctions between town and country continue to become blurred.

Even so, the Sunday School Treat was never the only outing for the children of many chapels. Those that had associated Scout and Guide movements would have their jamborees to attend, while children from village churches would be coached to appear at a rally or even an eisteddfod at one of the larger churches of the denomination, in a nearby town – perhaps the head of the circuit. Chapels in neighbouring villages would invite parties of children and grown-ups to their anniversaries, and once in a while there would be something a bit special – for example, when the London Missionary Society was commissioning a new ship for its work in

The Sunday School outing of the 1920s – by chara to Woolacoombe. (*Mrs M Stevens*)

the Pacific islands, *John Williams VI*, she visited various ports around the coast so that parties of children from the local churches could see her, and actually go on board. In the 1930s, when day-school outings were rare, this was quite an occasion. Witness, though, could be a part of Sunday School life in Wales, as in the North of England, and might involve a sort of treat as well. In one village in South Wales in the 1920s there were five chapels as well as the parish church, all well attended and with their Sunday Schools, and Whitsun Tuesday was the occasion of the 'School Walking', in which all the chapels took part. Each chapel's group was preceded by two men carrying a banner, and each had a hymn to sing, learned for the occasion. After the procession there was a 'tea of bread and butter, and madeira and fruit cake' for each of the chapel groups, in their respective vestries, followed by sports and games in a local field. And all this was quite separate from the *real* treat, which took place in the summer, when the children went in coaches to Barry Island for the day, singing on the way – 'We sang again on the way home, but not quite so lustily then, as we were tired and hot after a lovely day at the sea-side'.

122

Not that the children were the only people in the chapel to have an outing. In Essex, the Peculiar People used to hold a united thanksgiving service for the harvest, when virtually the whole sect was assembled at Chelmsford, filling the Corn Exchange for a set meal, and then moving en masse to Baddow Road Congregational Church for the afternoon service – surely an occasion that made as big an impact on the county town as any before or since the great days of that agricultural denomination. More decorously, chapels that were large enough and possessed a regular choir might have an annual choir outing, recognising the devotion of those who made sure to be 'up front' to lead the singing each Sabbath day. And, as we have seen, there would be journeys for the delegates to the county union meetings, the circuit events, and the national gatherings of the denomination, whether in London or some provincial city. As this kind of organisation developed, during the nineteenth century, many people in the villages found themselves making their first journeys away from home of any distance greater than that to their nearest market town.

Very often (though not in the example with which this chapter began) a Sunday School Treat included a sit-down tea, for which the premises of a sister chapel in the town to be visited would be borrowed. This would mean that tea could be brewed; maybe if there were funds available, a meal could be provided instead of the request that the children bring their own. Here we meet an aspect of chapel life that is often neglected; catering, for various events, could be a considerable responsibility – and, for local tradespeople, a useful source of income. Any self-respecting chapel would keep a set of china – plates, cups and saucers – and a few large enamel jugs; in addition, there would be that indispensable object, an urn. Maybe even two – large, made of polished copper, with a lid and, most important, a tap from which the tea could be drawn. Maybe the village football clubs could have a sausage supper, with beer in a bottle by every plate, but tea was the only refreshing liquid in chapel, made in the urn with water drawn from a boiler, and very likely carried in by the bucket from a well in the yard outside. However, strawberry teas were not unknown, in the more prosperous parts of the country, even if they sound more typical of the parish church.

This equipment had other purposes than providing for visiting parties, though, for the social life of the chapel throughout the years of rural poverty turned upon 'events', many of which would involve sitting down to a meal served on long trestle tables – themselves yet another essential piece of furniture. While the 1930s might see the churches in the nearby

Sunday School 'Walks' are often thought of as purely urban, but here the children of Potter Hanworth Methodist Chapel, near Lincoln, are ready to set out in 1911 or 1912. *(Mr J R Marshall)*

towns holding 'garden parties' to raise funds for redecoration or missionary enterprise, these might well seem too much like the 'fete' (often pronounced feet) that was associated with the parish church. Dissenters might attend the fete, but fund-raising for them was more likely to run to smaller events, and traditionally many of them would be held indoors.

The Harvest Festival might be associated with a 'harvest supper', followed by a sale of the produce. (Not all those prize marrows found their way to the local hospital!) Skills of auctioneering would not be unknown among the congregation, especially in the days when farm workers might well be acting for their master when they sold or bought stock at the local market. (The statutory requirement to hold an auctioneer's licence does not seem to have been enforced on these occasions.) In this way the surplus on the meal could be added to the product of the sale to make a useful contribution. Needless to say, no alcohol would be served at any of these events, but spirits could rise among the company, and the importance of the occasion would go well beyond the satisfaction of hunger.

124

In the smallest chapels the Harvest Festival was the most important event of the year – in a letter recalling the life of a Congregational chapel in Westmorland in the late 1920s we hear: 'We never had an outing. A small Christmas party perhaps, and once a year a missionary meeting with magic lantern slides and a talk on Mary Slessor and other missionaries. The main event of the year was the Sunday School Anniversary when we all got up and gave a recitation. A nerve-racking few minutes for a very shy girl. We also had of course a Harvest Festival and supper . . . The Harvest Festival was a very important event as the proceeds of the sale of fruit went towards raising the minister's salary – the Methodists always supported our events and we went back to theirs.'

After the sale of produce would come the preparations for the sale of work. 'Working parties' where women got together to produce saleable garments and household utilities would be supplemented by those who worked at home, and skills of embroidery came into their own now. Such groups might be called 'Dorcas meetings', with the biblical reference to the disciple raised from the dead by Peter in Acts Chapter 9, Verses 36–42, who made 'tunics and other garments'. Somewhat more extensive than a sale of work, though, would be a 'bazaar', which could be expected to

Harvest Festivals have real meaning in the country chapel – here at Meshaw, Devon, there is even the traditional vegetable marrow to be seen. *(Mrs M Stevens)*

A bazaar with a theme – at Brightlingsea, in Essex, the Congregational chapel took the local Foresters' Hall in 1927 for a *Rainbow Bazaar*; here is the opening scene.

include a wider variety of stalls – including produce, home-made cakes and so on, and perhaps even second-hand books. Refreshments, which might well consist of cups of tea and a few biscuits at a sale of work, could be expected to offer more substance at a bazaar, but what is more, there might very likely be some entertainment.

This could be a play by the children, with either a missionary or a temperance message, which had taken weeks to prepare, rehearse, and costume. The play might have a link with the theme of the event, in which case there could be quite extensive decorations. Of course, occasions of this kind would take place in the hall, if the chapel possessed one, or if not a hall would be hired for the day; either way, there would be work for the men, setting up the stalls, decorating the place with bunting or whatever, and – most important – arranging the platform.

For events of this kind require an element of formality, provided always by an opening ceremony. The buzz of activity comes to a close, as the little party sits around a table on the platform, itself adorned with flowers, and someone – probably the minister – calls upon the distinguished visitor to open the proceedings. Much can be learned about the nature of the chapel community now, for who has been persuaded to perform? Maybe someone local; in a small town, perhaps a councillor who is also a church member. Today it may be the vicar's wife – unthinkable not so many years ago. If the chapel is more or less isolationist, which may be the case in some of the evangelical sects, then it is more likely to be the pastor of a neighbouring cause; if it is a Methodist church, on the other hand, there will be the various circuit officers, and their wives, to call upon. Only if there is some special occasion, or if the object is to raise funds for missionary work, is there likely to be anyone who is completely strange to the assembled company – missionary activities in particular being able to call upon people home on furlough from the mission field.

Not that bazaars have always been occasions of friendship and light, for even chapel folk have their human failings. Whole families have taken themselves off to another congregation as a result of some quarrel, not infrequently arising from the social side of chapel life. We hear of two women who had 'done the teas' at every event for thirty years, though with an ill grace, refusing to do so ever again when they found a younger member of the chapel in 'their' kitchen one day, making a much-needed cup of tea. Contributions of cakes for the sale (or vegetables for harvest) may attract disapproval, and trouble can follow if any adverse remarks are overheard. We must remember, too, that to organise and run a bazaar or sale of work is demanding and exhausting, and resentment is bound to build up if someone is seen to be taking the credit for success who has not been bearing the heat and burden of the day.

At the lower end of the scale, though, there is still the jumble sale as a means of raising funds. What a world of difference lies between the niceties of the bazaar, with its dignitaries taking their place to open the proceedings, and the moment at a jumble sale when the doors of the hall open, and the waiting purchasers push their way in; scant ceremony for them, at most the parting with a few coins, if an admission charge is made. You need to be a different type of person to preside behind the trestle table loaded with part-worn clothing in a jumble sale from that which suffices to look after a stall at a bazaar or sale of work! Tougher, for one thing, and eagle-eyed too; quick to check the proffered money, and to give the correct change. But the efforts of the chapel folk, who have gone round collecting clothes and household articles from sympathisers, and then worked together the night before the sale, setting out the hall, and pricing the goods, all this can produce a rich reward in its contribution to the funds.

But if chapels have always run their jumble sales, as well as the more up-market events, you will not see them advertise that other attraction, the whist drive, that has been such a standby for various social organisations in the countryside, and certainly the chapel will have nothing to do with bingo. In 1943 the Congregational church at Ridgewell in Essex was divided on the question of whether or not darts should be played in the canteen provided for US Air Force men. Voting in church meeting was tied, with fourteen each way, but the minister used his casting vote to authorise a dartboard. Though other things may change, the nineteenth-century embargo on gambling, just as that upon alcohol, remains strong, and if this discourages some people from going to church, so be it. To see this as a social division characteristic of the late twentieth century is to forget the hostility of the nineteenth century, when evangelicals sought to make a stand against the evils they saw in their own society. And no one should doubt the pleasure that people get from the social aspects of chapel life.

The secular side of things being thus provided for, attention returns to those festivals that mark the passing of the chapel's year – the anniversaries. Biggest of these has always been the Sunday School Anniversary, when the crowded chapel has seen many people – parents and grandparents – who never attend it on any other day of the year. So long as the Sunday School tradition remained strong, the anniversary was the great event, perhaps next after Harvest Festival.

The idea of a sort of birthday party for the chapel families has an obvious attraction, but the anniversary was also a chance to 'involve the parents', in the days when getting rid of the kids for a while on Sunday afternoon was a social as well as a religious practice. And it was an occasion to be prepared for, with performances by the pupils – songs, recitations, missionary and temperance sketches, and of course the singing of hymns – often the learning of new ones. For the children it was a day for new clothes. (Anniversaries seem always to have taken place in early summer, probably fitting in the quietest period of the agricultural year, between hay and harvest.)

While performances at a bazaar or other winter entertainment would be in the church hall, or a secular building, anniversaries took place in the chapel itself, and on a Sunday. The morning service would be adapted to 'the needs of the children', with the hymns from the section of the hymn-

Epping Green Chapel.

— THE —

Anniversary

Services

Of the above will be held on

WEDNESDAY, JULY 26th, 1911

— When the —

Rev. J. CALVERT

Will Preach at 3.45 o'clock.

At 6.15, a

PUBLIC MEETING

Will be held, presided over by

John H. Boardman, Esq.
(Of Woodford.)

And the Revs J. CALVERT (Epping), A. D. BUTLER (Ware), and others are expected to address the meeting.

COLLECTIONS ON BEHALF OF CHAPEL FUNDS.

TEA at 5.15.   Tickets SIXPENCE each.

A. B. Davis Ltd., "Gazette" Office, Epping.

book headed 'For children and young people', and with the sermon probably giving way to a sort of extended children's address, or even being replaced by some form of presentation by the older children. Then in the afternoon there would be the central event of the day, when Sunday School was replaced by a chapel service, itself incorporating all the performances that had been rehearsed over the previous months. On this occasion the Sunday School superintendent would usually preside, though the minister would of course be present, and there would be visitors from other chapels as well, giving the whole thing a slightly competitive atmosphere.

Children and adults alike looked forward to the occasion. Here is one memory of it, from a Pennine village in the 1930s:

> . . . on the second Sunday in June the Sunday School Anniversary, still held today . . . celebrations (at) 10.30, 2.30 and 6.00. An invited minister, some well-known figure in the Baptist world, preaches the sermon. 'Teas provided for friends from a distance.' As children we all had new clothes for the occasion. The girls in particular were a joy to see, suddenly developing like a butterfly – what a difference a frilly dress, a large hat and her first 'silk' stockings made. For the boys the first long trousers, not until 13 or 14 years, was a wonderful occasion. For three or four weeks before the anniversary, afternoon Sunday school was transferred to the chapel in charge of the organist – a very capable musician who drilled us in the singing of the children's hymns – one for each service. The 'collection' was very important, the total being announced before the last hymn. The record I believe was in the early 1930s – £232, alas not equalled today in spite of inflation.

Anniversaries seem to have been a peculiarly nonconformist practice – Sunday School itself was unusual in the rural parish churches, and the equivalent festivals for Catholics were Saints' Days. What is more, the Sunday School Anniversary was often just the biggest and most expensive of several, the next being called the Church (or Chapel) Anniversary – a sort of birthday celebration, when there would be special services, with visiting preachers, and various representatives from the circuit or the county union. Perhaps less common would be the Minister's Anniversary, which might also fall on the nearest Sunday to the date of his induction, making it even more of a birthday.

All these events have one thing in common: they give a structure to the year that is otherwise missing in the traditions of dissent. For people whose forebears regarded Christmas as almost a pagan feast, and the observation of Saints' Days as unimaginably popish, there was a need for something to

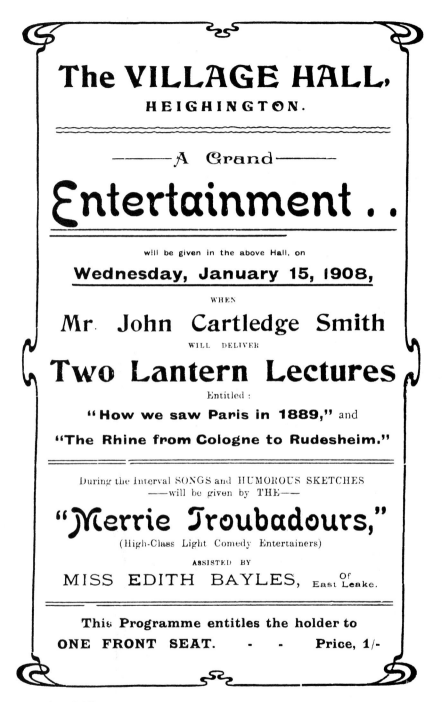

The VILLAGE HALL,

HEIGHINGTON.

———— A Grand ————

Entertainment ..

will be given in the above Hall, on

Wednesday, January 15, 1908,

WHEN

Mr. John Cartledge Smith

WILL DELIVER

Two Lantern Lectures

Entitled :

"How we saw Paris in 1889," and

"The Rhine from Cologne to Rudesheim."

During the Interval SONGS and HUMOROUS SKETCHES
——will be given by THE——

"Merrie Troubadours,"

(High-Class Light Comedy Entertainers)

ASSISTED BY

MISS EDITH BAYLES, Of East Leake.

This Programme entitles the holder to
ONE FRONT SEAT. - - Price, 1/-

Chapel folk might allow themselves some secular entertainment, too.

break the regularity of a form of worship that was also deliberately without ritual. After 1918 another special service might be that for Armistice Day, when in many small towns the mayor or council chairman would visit the different churches, year by year, in turn. Youth organisations connected with the chapel – more often Boys' Brigade than Scouts, though Girl Guides have a longer association with dissent – might have their special services, with blessing of banners and so on. In all these ways, too, the chapel made its presence known, for not only did posters advertise many such events, but local newspapers expected to cover them, too.

The repetitive nature of much rural life, measured by the changing seasons, found its echo in the repetitive pattern of chapel services; morning and evening, afternoon Sunday School, monthly communion, or some variation upon this theme. But while for some people no doubt the weekly attendance was sufficient, and the plain order of worship a comfortable foundation for their lives, we can see a different rhythm making itself felt over the year, to provide a continuing play of human activity, for which the chapel itself is the stage and scene.

Though the Church's year begins with Advent, this has never been a major celebration for dissent, and Christmas itself is perhaps more a festival of the ending of the year. New Year, though, has a strong tradition of celebration, not least in the Methodist connexions, with the 'Watch Night Service' offering an opportunity for re-dedication and hope. There follows the long procession of Sundays, when bad weather and illness can reduce numbers and the minister may feel it hardest of all to keep enthusiasm alive, until the 'pull' of Easter makes itself felt. But even in that 'low season', the choir may be rehearsing for an oratorio on Passion Sunday, and the routine of church meetings, deacons' meetings and working parties will continue. (Palm Sunday has not generally attracted the same observance in the nonconformist chapels as it has in the Catholic tradition, and there is very little mention of it in the contributions to this book.)

Good Friday observance has always varied from one part of the country to another, depending to some extent upon the regional differences in working practices; in most parts, the men would be working. Easter Day, though, has invariably been a major festival, with new clothes for the children (if they could possibly be afforded). Eighty years ago, in the memory of the author's mother, the children all had new balls to play with – a pagan survival that would have scandalised the good people of her little Essex town, if it had been understood!

From Easter through the summer and early autumn, events followed each other to give variety to chapel life. Even the end of winter had its observations, for many activities like the meetings of the Men's Fellowship would be wound up for the summer with some kind of concluding service. And all the time, the seasons brought – as they still do – the appropriate hymns, giving a further touch of variety when it becomes (hopefully) possible for the minister to choose one of the old favourites to open morning service, like 'Summer suns are glowing/Over land and sea'.

In chapels where there is a circuit organisation, there will be all the time the counterpoint of ministers and lay preachers as they work their way through the circuit plans. But in the chapels of old dissent, with settled pastorates, the summer sees a change, which may not be unwelcome to minister or people alike . The 'exchange of pulpits' will bring not just a new preacher, but a different thread of discourse, while it is a common practice for chapels of all denominations for visiting preachers of distinction to occupy the pulpit. And however small the chapel, it may from time to time be able to attract the chairman of conference or some other national figure, while the moderator will expect to preach in each chapel in the province at some time or another. Finally, the minister will be entitled to his or her family holiday during the summer, and while the circuit plan may allow for this, in other cases it will be necessary to arrange 'supply' preachers – often retired ministers living locally, or occasionally a minister from some distant city who is on holiday in the country.

The circuit system, incidentally, provides a longer-term rhythm, for it is usual to move ministers from one church to another at three-yearly intervals. Since this is a management decision, rather than the free choice of the congregations, there is a considerable amount of speculation among the chapels on the circuit, to say nothing of the tensions arising among the clergy concerned as the triennial period comes to a close. Villages being what they are, comments on the market bus will turn upon the minister's wife as much as the man himself.

To return to the changes of the year, summer will bring the annual rituals of anniversaries and treats, but it will also bring visitors to the pews, as members have family and friends to stay – all of them suitable for interested comment on the part of regulars. The summer is also a period when parties of students from the theological and Bible colleges take to the road, with a programme of evangelical services that will be associated with the chapels in the area of their mission; they too may lead the worship in some of the places where they stay. Complete strangers, though, have always been rare – except in seaside places, where chapel folk on holiday (in the days of the great British seaside stay) would expect to attend the local chapel of their own denomination, and hopefully to be made welcome.

Summer's end will see preparations for the Harvest Festival, and then the regular programme of winter meetings will be under way. In the country towns there will be the Armistice Day service to plan for, and the arrangements to be made for the annual bazaar. There will also be an 'annual meeting', attending perhaps by a minority, at which the officers of the chapel will present their reports, along with the audited accounts. Sometimes there may be a gift day; bring-and-buy sales may be a means of raising funds (though coffee mornings will be less common than they would be in connection with the parish church). At one time the children would be encouraged to bring packs of cotton wool and bandages, on Medical Missions Sunday, for despatch to the mission hospitals by way of the denominational missionary society; this had the intended effect of bringing mission work to the children as a reality.

Eventually the year's end comes with Christmas, but the evangelical tradition has always tended to be cautious about the celebration of Christ's Nativity. Even today, the separated communities, such as the Brethren, set their face against what they would regard as frivolity, thereby main-taining a true puritan tradition, and it must be admitted that Christmas is now inescapably a secular occasion, even for many who attend the chapel service as part of the day. But in the 'main stream' denominations there will be a tree with candles, and perhaps nowadays a crib, with once again the singing of familiar hymns and carols. And the Christmas morning service may be the one occasion when the minister is not expected to preach a sermon.

11

◇ The Chapels Today ◇

THE *Times* on 12 April 1986 published a letter describing 'a pastime which can be enjoyed in all weathers'. Not surprisingly related to the British climate, this was a 'chapel trail', which took place in North Wales. 'On foot or in the car, we hunted out the chapels and were astonished by the wealth of variety: square plan, side-wall façade, gable-ended auditorium, classic, Gothic, miscellaneous – all to be found within a small radius. Pink, blue, beige, stone, multi-coloured; Bethania, Moriah, Ebeneser, Siloam, Elim, Jerusalem; the permutations seem endless.' The writer quotes a publication of the National Museum of Wales, called just *Welsh Chapels*, and concludes: 'But hurry! Many of these buildings are redundant and fast disappearing; some of the best have gone already. The weather, for its part, continues its inexorable destruction of this remark-able feature of our heritage'.

The contrast between church and chapel, that we have come across in the English villages and country towns, has no parallel in Wales, where nonconformity has been the people's religion since the spread of Methodism and the evangelical revivals. The Anglican church retains a presence, as it does in Ireland, and seems to have been strengthened by disestablishment in 1920, but the Church in Wales has never had a basis in the 'gentry' that makes the Church of England what it is in rural communities; partly there is no Welsh equivalent of the English gentry, but partly too there is a fervour in Welsh religion that is but weakly reflected in the English.

This religiosity explains the abundance of chapels in Wales; the same small community may have not just more than one sect represented, as in parts of England, but also a distinction within one sect between Welsh-speaking and English-speaking congregations. There may be several chapels of the same sect, and language, within a community whose population, in England, would not justify more than, perhaps, a Methodist and an Evangelical Free Church, along with the parish church itself.

And all these buildings are the abodes of causes whose members have given their time, their effort and their money to build something, both physically and socially, that has meant more to them than their everyday concerns. Against this, the chapel trail as a pastime must seem wretchedly saddening; the shallow response of a secular society, where chapel-hunting is a way of amusing the family, given the vagaries of weather in the British Isles. The very names that are given as one of the component variables – Bethania, Siloam, Elim – were adopted as symbols of real faith, and considerable Biblical knowledge. A concordance is needed to elucidate them now*, and how many modern homes possess such a thing?

Yet the fact remains that we do live in what must appear to be an increasingly secular society, and even in Wales chapel-going is no longer the central cultural activity that it was when these chapels were being built. And that, too, is sad. Neither are abandoned chapels peculiar to Wales; it is just that there were so many more there to begin with. But, contrary perhaps to received opinion, the decay in chapel life is by no means a recent development; it is rather that the discovery of chapel buildings as objects of admiration is still rather new. The significance of our contemporary fixation for the archaeology of religion, as distinct from its spirit and purpose must be quite another matter.

Rural depopulation, starting in the late nineteenth century, is one cause of the change that has come over chapel life. The depression of the 1930s continued this in South Wales, and in both periods there was some benefit for urban churches and chapels. Adrian Hastings, looking at English Christianity in the 1920s, lays stress upon the spread of agnosticism in the upper levels of society, and it has often been observed that ideas take thirty years to work their way through to common ownership. There may be some coincidence here, as denominational loyalties seem to have tended to become looser from about the period of 'never had it so good' in the 1960s; this of course was not just a rural phenomenon, but it coincided also with a second period of rapid depopulation resulting from the mechanisation of agriculture. Even before that, though, many of the smaller causes had become vulnerable. Never strong in numbers, they could be dependent upon a few families, and the war often took its toll – at North Petherton, near Bridgwater, where the Wesleyan Methodist chapel had celebrated its centenary in 1932, it was forced to close when two of its younger members joined the Royal Air Force in 1939, causing what can only be described as a generation gap.

---

* – Bethania is of course Bethany; for Moriah see Genesis 22, 2; Ebeneser, 1 Samuel 4, 1; Siloam, John 9, 7, and Elim, Exodus 15, 27.

In the past thirty years, then, the country chapel has seen its membership decline; its young people leave for the towns; and its less committed supporters fall away. The same circumstances have applied in the parish church as well, and the incoming population of retired people or second-home owners from the towns have not brought any support to offset this decay; or not in sufficient numbers as to make much difference. Change of this kind can happen quickly; the Methodist (formerly Primitive) chapel at Hope's Gate in Shropshire celebrated its centenary in 1954 (a new Sunday School had been built only twenty years earlier), yet before another thirty years had passed, both school and chapel had closed, and today the building is just another curiosity for the chapel-hunter – and a place of personal sadness for those who once worshipped there, a sadness made more poignant by this final stanza from a celebration of its first hundred years:

> *Well, HOPE'S GATE is a century old!*
> *Its story is but partly told,*
> *For young and old, linked with this place,*
> *May write new chapters sweet with Grace.*
> *If 'names and sects and parties fall'*
> *And One Great Church include us all,*
> *Be HOPE'S GATE still a gate of hope*
> *To any who in darkness grope*
> *To find God's light, whose doubt or fear*
> *Might change to faith or courage here.*
> *And if our progress here seem slow*
> *At times, 'twill still be good to know*
> *In many places, hearts, and ways,*
> *GOD does GREAT THINGS. We'll sing His praise.*

Yet there are others that flourish. Perhaps an individual pastor may have given the congregation the lead they needed to grow; perhaps there will be a few devoted lay people, whose loyalty to a cause is matched by their faith in the tenets of their denomination; in any case, there are chapels in villages and small towns all over the country that have held their own, not just in population, but in community spirit too. It has been argued that the centralising trend that followed from Methodist reunion, and, more recently, from the formation of the United Reformed Church, has worked to the disadvantage of the small rural chapels, that for so long were supported by their neighbours in a circuit or a county union. The decision

At Hope's Gate, near Minsterley in Shropshire, the ladies' committee to build a Sunday School are posed for a group portrait, and in 1934 the foundation stone is laid. Sadly today the building is closed, along with the chapel itself. *(Mr & Mrs Overton/Wellington Journal)*

to 'stay out', whether by chapels of the Methodist persuasion or by those Independent (Congregational) causes that chose to stay out of the URC, would seem to have been a source of strength in many cases; perhaps because there is a challenge in 'going it alone'. And it is worth reflecting upon Gay's remark[*], concerning the Methodist reunion: 'The high initial hopes of union were not fulfilled and Methodism divided appears to have been more successful than Methodism united'.

Despite the various trends that have worked against the chapels, many survive and not a few flourish. Their background varies widely, from the Pentecostalist through the denominations of new and old dissent, to the Roman Catholic chapels, whose background is also in a form of dissent, and separation from the established religion of the nation. For many, though – perhaps for most – survival is not without problems, for it is the nature of the gathered church to depend as much as possible upon the

[*] – *The Geography of Religion in England*, p. 156.

The simplest building with the simplest message, Mosterton, in Dorset, near Crewkerne.

contributions of its members, whether directly in gifts of money or indirectly in money-raising efforts such as we looked at in chapter ten.

Demands upon the chapel's finances include the maintenance of the building (which to some extent can be dealt with by voluntary work), its lighting and heating (the latter being often quite expensive), and a certain amount for running expenses of a secretarial kind. But these form a small proportion when compared with the stipend of the minister or pastor – without whom the life of the chapel will become weakened, and its future uncertain. There will also be the need for a residence, which means either an allowance or the possession of a manse (with yet more running expenses), and it is difficult to see how a minister in a rural area can work without a car. Only the largest and best-endowed congregations can afford to be as generous as no doubt all would wish to be – but those are to be found in cities and prosperous suburbs; not in country towns and isolated villages.

The spread of chapels in the nineteenth century saw not a little down-right poverty among the dissenting clergy, and one of the efforts of the various national associations has been to require a minimum annual stipend and some standardisation as to payment of expenses. Along with this has had to go some system whereby the better-endowed churches can help the weaker ones (though this has been characteristic of the Methodist connexions and sects that adopted circuit organisation from a much earlier period). Without such mutual aid, and caring oversight at a regional or national level, it would be even more difficult for many of the chapels to survive.

Some have done so by grouping themselves together, so that one pastor can serve several causes, helped out by lay preachers, retired clergy living locally, or visiting ministers from the town. There is no doubt that the private car has made this a much more feasible strategy, for even in the days of adequate rural bus and train services, they did not necessarily connect the villages that needed to associate themselves most. The amount of walking that rural clergy of all denominations have done is something that would amaze the car-owning public of today.

Another answer to the problem may be the sharing of one minister by two chapels, in adjoining villages; this may mean having the Sunday service in the morning at one place and in the afternoon or evening at the other, unless, as with a group pastorate, other preachers can help out. The ultimate solution, increasingly to be found, is for congregations of different denominations to merge, enabling one pastor to serve both, and one building to be sold, with subsequent savings. It is a measure of the weakening of denominational boundaries that this should be found acceptable, but yet may it not be that the weakening of denominational and doctrinal loyalties has contributed to the frailty of the causes in the first place?

The ultimate problem, though, and it is not by any means a new one, is what should be done about the redundant buildings. The keen chapel-spotter soon develops an instinct for recognising them, and the number of alternative uses is not small. A word of warning, though: the mere presence of ecclesiastical windows is not sufficient to prove anything, because another casualty of the modern world has so often been the village school – and that might well have been itself a denominational building.

The problem is not new. When the United, the Primitive and the Wesleyan Methodists came together in 1932 to form the Methodist Church (still excluding the Independent Methodists, the Wesleyan

Reform Union, the Calvinistic Methodists and the Countess of Huntingdon's Connexion), there were numerous villages in which each of the
three connexions had a chapel. It was not always a happy matter to decide
which should remain as a place of worship for the united community, but
the problem was dealt with, if slowly – Gay records that by 1958 there were
only four per cent of Methodist chapels 'redundant' – and in the process,
not a few village bethels had been abandoned, with a good deal of sadness,
by the faithful few.

Like schools, chapels are not easily converted to other uses, and some
indeed have found a new and satisfactory use in the ownership of a
different congregation; an ideal arrangement, for the pews, pulpit, organ
and so on remain in use. At the other extreme is conversion of the building
to be used as some kind of warehouse, either for storage of goods or for
selling such things as carpets, furniture and antiques. (While there is one
example of a school being turned into a bus garage – at Ashen, in Essex –
this fate does not seem to have been met with by a chapel anywhere.)

Some of the simplest chapels, as we have seen, have stayed from their
exterior perspective as domesticated as they originally were; others (see
pages 42 and 48) could equally readily be mistaken for dwellings, were it
not for the notice-boards that indicate their function. Perhaps it is not
really as improper as it may seem for a chapel to be converted into a home,
since the early days of all the denominations have seen causes founded in
'cottage meetings'. Just what is possible must depend upon the architecture,
though, for some of the Gothic or Georgian styles hardly lend themselves
to homeliness. Even so, it must be admitted by the most diehard supporter
of rural nonconformity that it is better to see people living happily in a
former chapel building than to see it in a decayed, near-ruinous state,
forgotten by all and cared for by no one.

Here and there a chapel has been converted for a village hall (hopefully
never for use as a cinema); at Dedham in Essex the Congregational building
has been made into an arts centre – for the author, who once preached
there as a young man, it seems impossible to contemplate such a change of
use; a chapel, in its proper function, has an atmosphere at odds with the
attitudes of visitors to a secular occasion.

Pearson Thistlethwaite, a Yorkshire Quaker, has done some research
into the history of meeting houses in that county, of which he has
identified 203 as having been in use for public worship at some time or
another since 1647. Of these, he reports, 56 are still used regularly or
occasionally for Quaker worship; 50 still exist but in other uses; and 97

The chapel lives on – as a home. But this example at Alderton in Suffolk has kept its name.

have disappeared, completely or almost so. Here is his analysis of the uses to which the 'converted' ones have been put –

Private houses or flats	27
Church, Chapel or Sunday School	6
Garage or Workshop	5
Other commercial uses	5
Holiday Hostel	2
Arts Centre	1
Barn	1
Over-60 Club	1
Public House and Restaurant	1
Radio/TV Station	1
Theatre Store	1
Village Institute	1
Youth Club	1
Unoccupied (1986)	3
Total (this cannot be reconciled with the figure above because of multiple uses)	56

Not all of these are rural chapels, though far more of them would have been in the past than is the case today; the table does serve, though, to show what a range of alternative uses there are.

Pearson quotes one fascinating example – the former Friends' meeting house at Knapton, near Malton, which is now partly a Methodist chapel, and partly a barn. His detective work threw light on this, in the form of an entry in the diary of Elizabeth Robson, a 'ministering Friend', dating from 1815, and worth quoting in full for the light it throws upon the changes of history.

> 1815 Knapton. Isabella Tindall lives near in a spacious mansion, she is a member of our Society and some of her children, others of them not; one of the sons inclines to the Methodists. This family built a house for Friends to meet in and another for the Methodists, joined together, and divided by shutters, so that when either society wants the whole, each can be accommodated. There is also a steeple-house on their premises near to the other two places of worship.

An ingenious solution to an old problem, and one that could well be found useful today.

But perhaps after all it is best when a truly redundant chapel is actually demolished, to make way for everyday usefulness; however great the loss, if only to the built environment – the contribution of chapels and their surroundings to the village street, or to the mixture of styles in some country town, forms part of their value that should not be neglected. The persuasion of this book, though, is that the people make the chapel, not the building, so when they are gone, what is there that can remain?

12

◇ The View from the Chapel Door ◇

HERE is Bensusan, writing in the late 1940s, about his much-loved and
rapidly changing marshland – Mr and Mrs Orris have risen at six and
walked four miles by field paths and green lanes to the Peculiars' chapel at
Maychester, which is Bradwell-on-Sea. There they will spend their
Sabbath, taking part in three services, and eating the food they have
brought with them in the army hut nearby. It is morning service in the
little corrugated-iron building –

> Service lasted two hours, many brethren testifying to the joy that was in them
> and the temptations they had overcome, while few were in a hurry to sit down
> when they had taken the floor. 'I do wholly thank th' dear Lord', said one very
> old man, and he continued to say so until his wife laid a kind restraining hand
> in his and he subsided quietly, very pleased with his regular weekly con-
> tribution to the gathering. It was a congregation of late middle-aged or elderly
> folk, grace was not coming to the new generation.

The final words fall like lead upon the ears of those who have known the
faith of the chapels. But in the preface to the book* Bensusan, after
reflecting upon the conditions of life and work in the Essex marshland as
late as 1939, goes on: 'And yet in the better clad, better cared for
marshlanders who are entering on the second half of this century, I do not
find so many happy folk, young or old, as I met when it was about to open.'

It is easy to dismiss this as mere nostalgia, but Bensusan knew and loved
his marsh folk, and would never have pretended that their lives were
idyllic, or their damp and draughty cottages ideal for raising a family. Yet
what he said then rings true today, and not just in Essex – it is as true in
the 'sheers' that all right forward Essex men so despised; it is true in the
Westcountry and Wales; it is the loss of the old landmarks, in an increasingly
secular society, where urban values rule, even beyond the boundaries of
cities. The faith of Bensusan's chapel folk would hardly have come to terms

---

* – *Late Harvest*; Routledge & Kegan Paul, 1950.

Lonely on its hillside, above Snailbeach in Shropshire, the chapel retains its atmosphere of benediction still.

with *Songs of Praise* on television sets that they never lived to see.

What this amounts to is that the changed world of the country chapel reflects changes in British society that certainly have not yet run their course. But this still need not mean that the old values have been entirely lost, nor that the world may not still be viewed from the chapel door with a different and more stable perspective. For one thing should not be forgotten: there is no evidence of a 'golden age' of church- and chapel-going in the past, and 'chapel' has always been a minority persuasion. It was the Anglican poet William Cowper who wrote the eighteenth-century hymn whose lines still speak to the condition of the chapel congregation: 'Lord we are few, but Thou art near'.

Where the structural changes in rural society have been really sharp, as in those villages where almost every house, cottage and farm has been bought by 'incomers', chapel may suffer along with other basic aspects of life. Such villages may not lose just their bus service, but their post office and village shop – and the Church of England has been affected as much as the nonconformists by the second agricultural revolution. The problem is really severe where the former homes of villagers have become second homes, for then the place is dead until the weekend. But while there is often resentment at the arrival of newcomers who are young and prosperous, and whose work lies in our post-industrial economy, where you may not even have to commute to the local town, there may yet be benefits to follow from the change.

In many a country town, or in the villages that seem so 'unspoiled' to those who drive through them, it is tempting, for those whose roots are there, to write off such people as 'yuppies': tempting, but perhaps not very charitable. For religion is far from dead in Britain today, and the values of the Free Churches are still held in respect. So the country chapel may yet receive a providential renewal, and find a new opportunity for the future.

In the past, the country chapel has tended to be a socially conservative element in the community, committed to traditional values that have often seemed puritanical (though that is sadly to misread the nature of puritan thought). It is true that the world seen from the chapel door is in many ways narrowly defined, and that some of the dissenting chapels are the homes of either a slightly self-conscious evangelicism or of an inward-turning separation. (Some of the 'closed' sects that prefer rural anonymity to urban temptations actively discourage their members from allowing their names to appear on the electoral roll; if registered, they certainly are not permitted to vote.)

Yet the narrow perspective is one that gives a sense of certainty in a troubled world, and enables people to come to their own terms with modernity. Tradition; the very age of many chapel buildings; denominational loyalties that may no longer conflict with each other, but remain consciously important; these are elements of security. This is why there is often a certain reluctance to come to terms with new hymns, for the familiar ones convey continuity (as well as, all too often, having a depth of feeling and a foundation of doctrine that is lacking from the more recent effusions). Now that rural communities are subject to unprecedented change, the chapel, where it has survived, may be more important then ever.

But as we have seen, the barriers between the denominations that were so significant only a generation ago have been dismantled in many small towns and villages, and joint services as well as the sharing of a building by two congregations, are common today. This has been achieved without yielding supremacy to any one ecclesiastical structure. This perhaps gives the best hope for the future, for the experience of the Methodist reunion and that of the formation of the United Reform Church suggests that such reorganisations tend to have a weakening effect, by concentrating effort upon structural matters to the disadvantage of faith and witness.

Certainly we cannot expect the chapels to go back to the patterns of earlier generations, even though they too may carry a certain nostalgia for some of those who recall them. Here is one such recollection, to set against the typical Sunday of the late 1980s – Steep Lane Baptist Chapel, in the Pennines:

> Up to about 1939 my Sunday was – Sunday School 9.00 to 10.30, then service in chapel at 10.30 to 12.00 or sometimes 12.15. Sandwiches for lunch (30–40 people), tea provided in pint mugs for a penny. Sunday School 1.15, chapel 2.30 to 4.00. Then sandwiches again and finally a prayer meeting 6.00 to 7.00.

If this sounds a gruelling experience for the day of rest, hear what our contributor says of it:

> The central part of the service was the sermon. 3 and 4 year olds and even 10 year olds can hardly be expected to understand a sermon, but we were there, and by the age of 13 or 14 I had become a 'sermon enthusiast' and still am today.

The village once had five Free Churches – as well as the Baptists, there were three Methodist chapels (Wesleyan, Primitive and United), and one Congregational. Now only the Baptist remains. No doubt the Sunday services are less of an obstacle course than some may have found them in the 1930s, for the country chapel has changed along with the rest of society. But it is still there, in many small towns and villages, and folk still go to meeting on Sundays.

So let us slip into our pew in some chapel for morning service. There is a buzz of conversation, quiet but persistent, but we can ignore it as we sit and bow our heads for a few moments in devotion. The sun pours through windows of plain glass; the pew is hard and comfortless; before us there is the pulpit, the communion table, the chairs for the choir; beyond them there rises the organ. Then the voluntary begins, and conversation fades, until the minister enters, following the choir, and all is still. The call to worship is followed by the announcement of the first hymn (its number shown on the board, high on the wall before us), and as the organist plays over the tune we rise with the choir as he starts the last line.

Somehow that first hymn establishes for us the purpose for which we have come – communal worship has begun. Prayers and scripture readings

The oldest – and the loneliest – of all. St Cedd's Chapel (St Peter ad Muram, in the parish of Bradwell-juxta-Mare, Essex), on the foundations of the Roman fort of Othona. Here is where it all began.

with more hymns follow; the collection is taken, and we stand for its dedication; standing or sitting, we are sharing something that we all understand, yet few perhaps could describe. And all this leads to the high point of the service, as we settle down, in a silence as communal as any of our actions, to listen to the sermon – the preaching of the Word. The minister knows how much his flock value the sermon, and he has something to say that leaves us 'with something to think about' – the ultimate praise for the teaching ministry. Let us not have any doubts as to how the congregation are following what is said; they may not all be well able to express themselves, but they have been listening to sermons all their lives, and they will all of them take something they need from fifteen to twenty minutes of concentrated attention.

Soon the sermon ends, and the final hymn is announced – today is not a 'sacrament Sunday', so the service will not go on to the simple ritual of communion. We began the service with Isaac Watts' celebration of communal worship – versifying Psalm 122:

149

> *How pleased and blest was I*
> *To hear the people cry,*
> *Come, let us seek our God today!*

– and now we close with Charles Wesley's dedicatory hymn:

> *Ready for all Thy perfect will,*
> *My acts of faith and love repeat,*
> *Till death Thy endless mercies seal,*
> *And make my sacrifice complete.*

Following that, the blessing comes to round off this hour that has been set aside from secular affairs. We have indeed shared in an act of worship that could as well be that of an urban or a suburban church or chapel, for at this level there is no real distinction between them. But as we sit, with bowed heads once more, making our final devotions before the closing voluntary starts, perhaps there is something in the silence of the peace of the fields – perhaps birdsong or animal cries float through the high

150

windows. Perhaps even the cry of sheep, to point up a sermon on the Good Shepherd.

And then, the voluntary under way, we join the people moving to the door, where the minister waits to shake hands – it's a lovely morning and surely we feel the more part of it because the chapel is too. Surely the view from the chapel door was never better.

◆ Bibliography ◆

In a book that makes no serious pretensions to scholarship, the sources that have been used are certainly not exhaustive. For the early story I went back to an old and familiar companion, *A Popular History of the Free Churches*, by C Silvester Horne (James Clarke & Co, 1903). Books that I had to hand all the time were John Bishop's *Methodist Worship in Relation to Free Church Worship* (Epworth Press, 1950); John D Gay's *The Geography of Religion in England* (Duckworth, 1971); Kenneth Lindley's *Chapel and Meeting Houses* (John Baker, 1969); *Hallelujah! – Recording chapels and meeting houses* (Council for British Archaeology, 1985); and David A Barton's *Discovering Chapels and Meeting Houses* (Shire Publications, Aylesbury, 1975). Towards the end of the work I was also able to refer to Adrian Hastings' pathbreaking book, *A History of English Christianity 1920–1985* (Collins, 1986), and I wish I had had it by me sooner.

Pamphlets and specialist works that I have used are too numerous to list, but I would like to thank all those friends, whose names appear below, who sent me so many of them. Perhaps a few may be mentioned, to stand representing my gratitude to all: *Those Hundred and Fifty Years: A Ter-Jubilee History of the Strict Baptist Church at Aldringham, Suffolk* by George T Botwright (1962); *The Story of Gressenhall Methodist Church or God's Cottage* by Cyril Jolly (1985); *Little Baddow United Reformed Church – A History* by Revd Dr R Buick Knox (1976); *The Northwood Story – The History of High Legh Independent Methodist Church 1783–1983* by John A Dolan (1983); *They Came to Ridgewell* by Frances L Cleeves (1987) and *Horningsham Chapel – The Story of England's Oldest Free Church* by Albert E Barton (revised edition, 1979). Copies, or photocopies of all these have been deposited in Dr Williams's Library.

One or two other books I must mention are Cyril Jolly's *History of the East Dereham Methodist Circuit* (Geo. R Reeve, Wymondham, n.d. – c 1956); Bill Parry's *Peculiar Preachers* (New Life Publications, Caernarfon, n.d.); and Mark Sorrell's *The Peculiar People* – a wonderful book that succeeds in being both devotional and scholarly (Paternoster Press,

Exeter, 1979). A word of greeting also to an old friend, Professor Donald Davie, for his contribution, *A Gathered Church* (Routledge & Kegan Paul, 1978), which more than anything else enabled Free Churchmen to take a proper pride in their cultural inheritance. Finally, three academic papers that I found valuable: D W Bebbington, 'The City, the Countryside and the Social Gospel in Late Victorian Nonconformity' (*Studies in Church History*, 16, Oxford, 1979); Roger Homan, 'The Society of Dependents: A Case Study in the Rise and Fall of Rural Peculiars' (*Sussex Archaeological Collections*, 119, 1981); and 'The Brethren' – A Recent Sociological Study', by Bryan Wilson of All Souls College, (Allaby Press, Melbourne, Australia), which Dr Wilson kindly provided for me in photocopy.

⋄ Acknowledgements ⋄

In turning to the pleasant task of acknowledging all the help that I have been given – and all the new friends I feel I have made – in the course of writing this book, I can only list all the names, for it would be impossible to identify each contribution, and yet every one of them has given something. If this book 'comes to life' for the reader, as I hope it does, then that is due to the letters and documents that have been sent to me, as a result of my requests published in the denominational periodicals at the start of the work (and may I thank those editors, too). So here are the names of all the people who, in different ways, have helped me to write a book, and given me their blessing on the way: First, the librarian and staff of Dr Williams's Library, and Mr Donald P Raine, Bookseller, of Shipley, who helped me to find texts that I needed. Then my many new friends and correspondents, and let me say that all the letters and papers that I have received have been deposited in Dr Williams's Library, for others to use: Dr David Bebbington, Mr J Bensusan Butt, Roy Bentley, Bert Bridges, Baron G Britton, David Brown (of Weeley), Edith Brown (of Buckland Brewer), Mrs Dorothy I Butler, Jo Campbell, Vicky Carter, Mrs J Chadwick, Miss D Charlesworth, Trudy Christen, Mrs I Clark, Pastor Frances Cleeves, Mr T A Dewing, John A Dolan, Phyllis M Edwards, Professor John Ferguson, Leslie J Francis, Vera Geddis, Harold Hanson, Catherine Harkham, John Hickman, Dr R E Homan, Cyril Johnson, Cyril Jolly, Dr R Tudur Jones, Mrs Doris McGowan, Leonard J Maguire, Mrs Doris L Mann, Hilda Marsh, J R Marshall, Mr Nathaniel Micklem, J H Mills, Christopher Monro, L Mary Neave, Dr G Nelson, Mr J F Newth, Mr & Mrs Overton, Revd G H Paton, Harry Pallett, Pastor R G Prime, John Quincey, Sadie K Ritchie, Elsie Ritson, Revd Mrs A M V Robinson, Mrs M Robinson (of Hereford), Mr E Roscoe OBE, Mr A D Rowland, Eric & Joyce Rutter, Arthur & Molly Smith (of Haywards Heath), Mr F G Smith (of Bedford), Mr W R Smith (of Devizes), Mark Sorrell, Mrs A Spender, Jack Squire, Mr Christopher Stell, Muriel Stevens (of Earley), Mrs M Stevens (of Bude), Winifred Stokes, Pearson Thistlesthwaite,

_• Acknowledgements •

Revd Dr Harold Tonks, Mrs V Townsend, Joyce Tristram, Mrs Mary J E Walker, H Kathleen Wardle, Mrs Muriel West, John Whitehorn, Dr B R Wilson, James Wilson (of Reading), Ruth M Wilson (of Henley-on-Thames) and Mr R J Wood. And then, as with *The Country Bus*, I have had the pleasure of sharing in the making of this book with David St John Thomas, and the benefit of his discrimination and encouragement; as with that book, too, I have happily to acknowledge the contributions of Eric Axten and Jim Bray in making the drawings. Finally, my thanks to Revd Elsie Chamberlain for contributing the foreword are combined with appreciation of her understanding that this is not just an antiquarian study.

Closer to home, my family have given me every encouragement – and that includes Barney and Layla, the Boxers, and Connor the Wolfhound, who have dropped into the study from time to time, and Sacha the Spaniel and Nelson the Poodle, who have happily slept there, undisturbed by the sound of the typewriter. In a deeper sense, more than I can easily identify must be the contribution of my wife, Paddy, whose Catholic faith complements so well my own inherent dissent. It is to her that this book is dedicated.

⬧ Index ⬧